Study Skills for Speakers of
English as a Second Language

Palgrave Study Skills

Authoring a PhD
Business Degree Success
Career Skills
Critical Thinking Skills
e-Learning Skills (2nd edn)
Effective Communication for
  Arts and Humanities Students
Effective Communication for
  Science and Technology
The Exam Skills Handbook
The Foundations of Research
The Good Supervisor
How to Manage your Arts, Humanities and
  Social Science Degree
How to Manage your Distance and
  Open Learning Course
How to Manage your Postgraduate Course
How to Manage your Science and
  Technology Degree
How to Study Foreign Languages
How to Write Better Essays (2nd edn)
IT Skills for Successful Study
The International Student Handbook
Making Sense of Statistics
The Mature Student's Guide to Writing (2nd edn)
The Personal Tutor's Handbook
The Postgraduate Research Handbook (2nd edn)
Presentation Skills for Students

The Principles of Writing in Psychology
Professional Writing (2nd edn)
Researching Online
Research Using IT
Skills for Success
The Study Abroad Handbook
The Student's Guide to Writing (2nd edn)
The Student Life Handbook
The Study Skills Handbook (3rd edn)
Study Skills for Speakers of English as
  a Second Language
Studying the Built Environment
Studying Business at MBA and Masters Level
Studying Economics
Studying History (3rd edn)
Studying Law (2nd edn)
Studying Mathematics and its Applications
Studying Modern Drama (2nd edn)
Studying Physics
Studying Programming
Studying Psychology (2nd edn)
Teaching Study Skills and Supporting Learning
Work Placements – A Survival Guide for Students
Writing for Nursing and Midwifery Students
Write it Right
Writing for Engineers (3rd edn)

Palgrave Study Skills: Literature

General Editors: John Peck and Martin Coyle

How to Begin Studying English Literature
  (3rd edn)
How to Study a Jane Austen Novel (2nd edn)
How to Study a Charles Dickens Novel
How to Study Chaucer (2nd edn)
How to Study an E. M. Forster Novel
How to Study James Joyce
How to Study Linguistics (2nd edn)

How to Study Modern Poetry
How to Study a Novel (2nd edn)
How to Study a Poet
How to Study a Renaissance Play
How to Study Romantic Poetry (2nd edn)
How to Study a Shakespeare Play (2nd edn)
How to Study Television
Practical Criticism

Study Skills for Speakers of English as a Second Language

Marilyn Lewis and Hayo Reinders

palgrave
macmillan

First published 2003 by
PALGRAVE MACMILLAN
Houndmills, Basingstoke, Hampshire RG21 6XS and
175 Fifth Avenue, New York, N.Y. 10010
Companies and representatives throughout the world

PALGRAVE MACMILLAN is the global academic imprint of the Palgrave Macmillan division of St. Martin's Press, LLC and of Palgrave Macmillan Ltd. Macmillan® is a registered trademark in the United States, United Kingdom and other countries. Palgrave is a registered trademark in the European Union and other countries.

ISBN-13: 978–1–4039–0026–5 paperback
ISBN-10: 1–4039–0026–4   paperback

This book is printed on paper suitable for recycling and made from fully managed and sustained forest sources. Logging, pulping and manufacturing processes are expected to conform to the environmental regulations of the country of origin.

A catalogue record for this book is available from the British Library.

Printed and bound in China

10   9   8   7   6   5
13 12 11 10 09 08

To Wynford, the eldest of the next generation.
M.L.

To my best friend, Kim Youn Soo, forever.
To my parents, for everything.
H.R.

Contents

List of Tables

Acknowledgements

The authors and publisher would like to thank the following for permission to reproduce copyright material:

Figure 1: 'Documents for university enrolments': taken from the University of Auckland's website.

Figure 2: 'Choosing important language skills': taken from the English Language Self Access Centre's Electronic Learning Environment, the University of Auckland.

Figure 3: 'Choosing your current level and your goal level': taken from the English Language Self Access Centre's Electronic Learning Environment, the University of Auckland.

Figure 4: 'Writing a problem and a solution statement': taken from the English Language Self Access Centre's Electronic Learning Environment, the University of Auckland.

Figure 6: 'Searching for materials': taken from the English Language Self Access Centre's Electronic Learning Environment, the University of Auckland.

Figure 7: 'List of scientific topics': taken from www.yahoo.com, p. 123.

Figure 8: 'Yahoo's advanced search page': taken from www.yahoo.com.

Figure 11: 'A course website's menu structure': taken from www.blackboard.com.

Figure 12: 'The course website': taken from www.blackboard.com, p. 70.

Figure 13: 'Course website, student tools page': taken from www.blackboard.com, p. 71.

Several examples have been taken from the English Language Self Access Centre (ELSAC) at the University of Auckland and have been written by ELSAC and University of Auckland staff, including Rosemary Wette, John Tomlins, Shuhei Hidaka, Rebecca Tsang, Marilyn Lewis and Hayo Reinders.

Introduction

This book is for students who speak English as a second language and who are planning to study at an English-speaking university. There is some information you need before enrolling, such as details of the IELTS and TOEFL examination, there are chapters for students doing a first degree, and there is some information for postgraduate students. We have tried to write in straightforward language at a level you would need to study at university.

The book is based on our own experiences as teachers and as students in various countries. Both of us have gone overseas for university study and know what it is like to study in a second language. We have also listened to the stories of university students who speak English as a second language, and to their teachers. Their experiences and ours helped us write this book.

Because this is a reference book, and because different chapters will be of interest at different times, readers can turn to whatever section suits them. First have a look at the Contents pages and see if a chapter fits your interest, such as the chapter on 'Lectures', which gives advice on listening and notetaking. If you don't find exactly what you want in the Contents list, then turn to the index. Here you can look up a topic you want to know more about, such as *notetaking* or *tutorials* or *homestay*. Use the index for new words you hear everyone use at university, such as *Faculty* or *discussion boards*. The other place to look for word meanings is in the Glossary. This section is arranged like a small dictionary, giving you a short, quick meaning of terms that are used through the book. If you want to know more about the meaning of any of these words then you can go back to the index to find the page where each is explained in more detail.

We hope that you find what you want somewhere in these pages. Although we have tried to give you the big picture, we know that there are differences from one university to another. For a more detailed picture you can read the books and websites suggested throughout the chapters. We hope that wherever you are reading this book and whatever stage of your university life you have reached, you will find the ideas helpful. We would be pleased to hear from you if this book has been useful to you or if you think some of the information should be changed. Any feedback is welcome! You can email us at studyskills@hayo.nl. Happy reading!

Marilyn Lewis

The University of Auckland   Hayo Reinders

Part I
Getting Organised

Introduction

If you are interested in studying at a university overseas but still have a number of questions, the first three chapters of this book take you through three important stages. The first stage is deciding where to go and how to make sure that your English language is at a suitable level. Then comes the second stage, when you plan a programme that suits you and that fits a particular university's programmes. The third stage is for students whose English needs improving.

If you have already moved through all these stages then you are ready for Part II of this book.

1 Pre-departure decisions

All over the world students are changing countries for their university studies. This chapter is written for people who are at the first stage of planning. They have already decided to go but are still thinking about which country and university would be right for them. Part of the decision depends on which courses are offered at which university but students also choose their place of study because they like the country, its language, and/or its culture.

This chapter answers the following questions:

- How do students choose their university?
- How can students get scholarships?
- What tests and examinations measure students' English levels?

▶ Which university?

Why do people study overseas?
We asked students why they had left their country to study at an English-language university in another part of the world. Here are some of their answers.

Student 1
Adventure! I had never lived overseas and always wanted to. That's why, when I got a scholarship to go to another country, I jumped at it! I always wanted to go to Europe, so I went to study in Great Britain for a year and visited the Continent in my holidays.

Although this student mentions adventure as the motivation, having a scholarship must also have been an important point. Later in this chapter you will read about applying for scholarships.

Student 2

> *I actually had to go overseas to get into a university. I didn't want to go but in Korea it is very difficult to get into a good university. Your grades have to be very high, but mine weren't. In the United States it was much easier for me to enter university so I decided to go there.*

As you can see, for this student practical reasons were the reason for going overseas.

Student 3

> *For me the main reason was to learn English. My parents wanted me to get to know other cultures and to learn English well because this would be good for my career. I think I have learned a lot from living in another country.*

This student had language reasons as well as study reasons for changing countries. If you share this student's aim, read about making friends and about homestays (in Chapter 11).

Student 4

> *I had little choice. My subject, petrochemical engineering, is not very well developed in my country and I had to go overseas to study it.*

This student probably did some searching on the Internet to find exactly the right university for this specialised subject.

Student 5

> *I went to have a break really! I had finished my studies in computer science and decided to do a postgraduate diploma in Australia. One year of beaches, going out and a bit of studying sounded great – and it was!*

This comment goes to show the mixture of reasons people have for overseas studies. It sounds from the words 'a bit of studying' that the student chose a course that was not too difficult for him or her.

Some of the reasons we have seen so far include the following.

- Their subject is taught better elsewhere.
- They want to learn more English.
- They are interested in other cultures.
- It is difficult to get into university in their own country.
- They will get a better job.
- They like the idea of travelling to another country.

Once students have decided to go away, the next thing to think about is where?

How do students decide where to go?
Next we asked students some questions about how they decided on the country and the university for their study. You could try answering the questions for yourself.

Student 6
> *Money was an important reason for me to study in New Zealand. University fees are lower there than elsewhere and the cost of living is much lower too. Also we had a good exchange rate.*

This student is, very sensibly, thinking about money but of course exchange rates can change over three or four years of study.

Student 7
> *I ended up studying at a different university from the one I intended. The university I wanted to enrol for turned down my application because of my grades. Another university in the same city was much easier to get into and I therefore ended up there.*

Here is a good idea. You needn't change your mind about a particular country or even a city just because you have a 'no' answer from one place.

Student 8
> *I would have loved to study at Oxford or Cambridge or a place like that, but I just can't afford it!*

We call this student a realist. Dreams are great but the real situation may be different.

Student 9
> *Many of my friends went to the States and I have an uncle who lives there, so I went there too.*

Having support from friends and family is very important, as we see in Part III.

In summary, here are the reasons people gave for studying at a particular university.

Quality
Some universities have a very good 'name' and are famous around the world. However, as well as thinking about the 'name', think about whether the university you have in mind is strong in the subjects you want to study. Some universities are famous for particular departments.

The cost

The cost of going to another country includes much more than the university fees. What the cost of living will mean for you and your family depends partly on the rate of exchange between the two countries and of course this rate can change from time to time.

Entry requirements

The 'entry requirements' are the grades and qualifications you need to take the course of your choice. For example, if you want to become a (medical) doctor, some universities want you to prove that you are very good at English and maybe that you have taken subjects like English and History in high school. There is more on this topic later in the chapter.

The country

Some students choose a country first and then a university. Maybe a family member has already studied there and enjoyed meeting the people and learning about the culture. Perhaps, like Student 5 who went to Australia, they like the climate in a particular country. Perhaps they have seen photographs of the country which suggest it has a beautiful landscape.

Meeting students from your country

Another reason for choosing a particular country is because many people from your country are there. In that case you will be able to speak your own language sometimes and find food that is familiar.

Visas

One big question to think about is how easy it is for someone with your passport to get a visa to study in a particular country. As world events change, so do the regulations. Ask at the Embassy of the country where you hope to study. Sometimes there are special arrangements between two countries or even between two universities.

Available places

Sometimes it is very difficult to get a place on a particular course, such as Law, even though you have all the entry requirements. Popular courses or courses where equipment is needed, such as Fine Arts, often limit their places. If you are not accepted for the course you want at the university of your choice you could:

- try another country;
- try another university in the same country;

- try a different course;
- wait another year and try again when your grades are higher.

Course dates
Year-long courses usually start in September in the Northern Hemisphere and in March in the Southern Hemisphere. However, many courses have a semester system which means you can start any course every six months or even at a Summer School.

The university site
Perhaps the environment is important to you. Do you like to live near the city or in a quieter, more peaceful area? If you want to travel to town sometimes, how easy is the transport? Some universities have more than one campus.

Finding out more
To find out as much information as you can about particular countries, universities and courses, try one of these ideas:

- Go to the university's website.
- Ask people who have been there.
- Find out what people in your future profession think about a degree from that university. Is it easy to find work with that degree?
- Although it is expensive, some families visit the universities they are interested in for their sons and daughters.

Here are some Internet addresses to help you in your search:

www.unofficial-guides.com

This site has information about universities in Great Britain.

iiswinprd03.petersons.com/ugchannel

This is one of many sites with information about universities in the United States.

www.thegoodguides.com.au

This site lists and compares universities in Australia.

▶ Applying for a scholarship

For many students, studying overseas is very expensive, probably much more than it would be in their own country. As we mentioned earlier, in addition to the fees there is the cost of living, which includes housing, food, travel and clothing. These too may be much higher than at home. Students find the money for all these costs in many ways, and one way is to have a scholarship. A scholarship is money given to a student by a university or a government or some other place, to help with study costs. This section discusses scholarships and how to apply for them.

Types of scholarships
A scholarship may pay for any or all of these:

- course fees;
- living costs;
- travel to and from the new country;
- research costs.

You may be surprised to learn that there are many different types of scholarship. Here are examples from students who talked to us:

1. Government scholarships for:
   the children or grandchildren of soldiers;
   people of a minority ethnic group;
   students whose parents have a low income;
   students from a particular country.

2. Business scholarships for students who
   plan to be employed in business;
   are already working in the company that gives the scholarship.

3. University scholarships for students who
   have done well in the first year of their studies;
   have some physical problem;
   want to finish a piece of research;
   belong to an ethnic group which the university wants to encourage.

In summary, there are scholarships for undergraduate and postgraduate studies, for specific areas of study (e.g. computing or medicine) and sometimes for students from certain countries. There are scholarships for women, for people of certain ethnic backgrounds, and many more. Ask about one that could apply to you.

Also, you want to know whether the scholarship comes with conditions such as these or others:

Applicants must agree to return and work in [*name of country*] for a minimum of three years after graduating.

On graduating, the scholarship holder must work for [*x company for y years*] or refund the scholarship in whole or in part.

Students who receive this postgraduate scholarship must agree to let [*the company that gave the scholarship*] use the results of their study.

Where to find out about scholarships

There are several places to go for information about scholarships, both in your own country and in the country you are going to. If you have studied before, then your own university is the best place to start looking. The Scholarships Office will have information about scholarships that are available from companies, your own government, other governments and other universities. Often this information is also on the website of the university where you plan to study and there will probably be an office that helps students apply for scholarships.

A good place to start looking is one of these sites:

www.iefa.com

Here, international students can search for scholarships by area of study, by the country of origin, by the region where they want to study, or by the name of the university.

www.isoa.org

This site is specifically for international students already living in the United States.

www.globalgrant.com

Although this site charges a fee to help you find a scholarship, this kind of service may be useful when you don't have access to a university or if your university does not have someone to help you with your scholarship.

As well as scholarships, your own government may sponsor people to study overseas by paying travel expenses as well as tuition fees. A good place to look is at the website of the Ministry of Foreign Affairs or the Ministry of Education.

There are also scholarships given by international organisations such as the United Nations. These are usually awarded to students from certain countries or for students who cannot afford the tuition fees.

How to apply for a scholarship

The first thing is to make sure you are eligible (can apply). As we saw earlier, eligibility depends on your age, nationality, qualifications, work experience etc. When you have decided that the scholarship is right for you, you must check what types of documents you need to send in.

As with your general university application, applying for a scholarship can take time. Have a look at Figure 1, an example from one university. As you can see, you need to send different kinds of information. For example, one of the things that you normally need is a recommendation. It is not clear in this example what kind of recommendation they want but a recommendation is usually a letter saying one or more of the following.

- You are a very good student.
- You have experience studying at another university.
- You have done or are doing research in a certain field.

A recommendation needs to show that the person who recommends you is confident that you will be a successful student.

Sometimes you also need an *endorsement*, which is different from a recommendation. Usually you get one from the Ministry of Education in your country, saying that your country wishes to support you in your studies.

Application forms

Application forms need to be written very carefully and clearly. Perhaps it's best to do your first draft on a photocopy. Also, if you want to make sure you don't make any language mistakes, have your application checked by someone else. One thing to get right is in what order to put your names (family name or surname, and given names). English names, as you probably know, are spoken with the surname last, but on forms the surnames usually go first.

Sometimes there is space on the form to say why you are applying for the scholarship. In that case it is very important to be clear and enthusiastic.

Required Documents

In addition to completing and returning the appropriate application forms, scholarship applicants must provide the following documents:

- Certified copy of passport or birth certificate.
- Certified copy of degree certificates.
- Certified copy of tertiary academic transcripts.
- International English Language Testing System (IELTS) or Test of English as a Foreign Language (TOEFL) scores. The IELTS test must be the academic module and the TOEFL test must include TWE [Test of Written English] or Essay Rating.

Minimum Postgraduate Requirements

IELTS: Overall band 6.5 plus no band less than 6.
TOEFL: 575 plus TWE 4.5.
TOEFL (computer-based): 233 plus Essay Rating 4.5.
Note that some postgraduate programmes may have higher requirements.

- At least three letters of recommendation from people who have known the applicant in a professional capacity, such as past or present lecturers, employers, supervisors or work colleagues.
- Curriculum vitae, stating the applicant's education background and work history.
- Evidence of annual salary, such as certification from your employer or the government taxation department (if applying for an Asian Development Bank Postgraduate Scholarship).
- Certified Graduate Management Admission Test (GMAT) scores (if applying for admission to the Master of International Business programme).

Doctoral applicants must also provide:
- Evidence of research experience, such as an extract of your Master's thesis or publications.
- Doctoral research proposal.

Documents that are in a foreign language must be accompanied by certified English translations.

Figure 1   Documents for university enrolments

You need to show what your plans are and how this scholarship can help you.

Here are two examples, the first showing how NOT to do it.

I like computers and therefore I want to study computing. I want to go to New Zealand because it is a beautiful country.

Now, here is an example of how to do it.

> I have studied computer science in my country for three years and have obtained a Bachelor's degree. I am very eager to continue my studies by starting a Master's programme so that I can specialise in artificial intelligence. This is an important field and I believe that with this qualification I will be able to contribute to the technological knowledge in my country. The reasons why I want to study at your university are that computing science there has a very good international reputation and in addition the living costs are not so high. With the help of a scholarship I will be able to finish my Master's within one year.

As you can see, this student writes clearly, listing several reasons for applying for a scholarship. Obviously, a well-planned support statement has a better chance of success.

If all this information makes a scholarship seem very far away, remember, someone has to get it. Why not you?

▶ Finding out your English level

Before you can plan ways of improving your English, you want to know exactly what you do well and what needs improvement. One way to find out your present level is to do a diagnostic test. This is a type of 'needs analysis', which looks at your English language and tells you your strengths and weaknesses. From this you know what you need to work on.

We are going to look at one type of needs analysis, which has questions for you to answer. This example is made to be used on the computer but you can easily do it yourself using pen and paper.

Step 1
As you can see in Figure 2, it starts by asking how important a number of skills are to you. You choose from 'not important' to 'very important'. Start writing down all the skills you can think of. The example lists a number, but you can add others. For instance, as one of your skills you could write down 'writing summaries' or 'giving presentations'. Then write down how important each one is, as in the example.

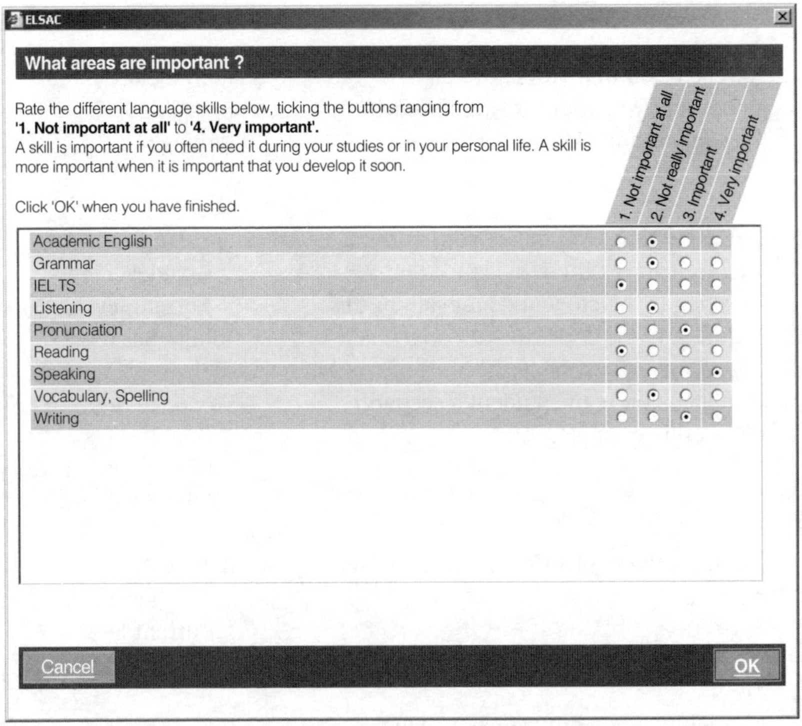

Figure 2   Choosing important language skills

Step 2

The next step is to decide your present level and the level you would like to reach (your goal level). In the example in Figure 3 the computer has selected only the skills that the student has chosen as important or very important. You can do the same.

Step 3

In the third step the computer calculates how important each skill is for you and tells you which skill you should work on first. You can do the same thing without the computer, by using this simple formula:

A

For each skill that you chose as 'important' you count 3, and for each 'very important' skill, count 4.

Pronunciation = 3
Speaking = 4
Writing = 3

B

Take your goal level minus your current level for each of these skills.
Speaking is the student's first skill in this example.

Speaking:
   Goal level is 8
   Current level is 6
   Total = 8 − 6 = 2

Pronunciation is the student's second skill in this example.

Pronunciation:
   Goal level is 8
   Current level is 6
   Total = 8 − 6 = 2

Writing is the student's third skill in this example.

Writing:
   Goal level is 9
   Current level is 5
   Total = 9 − 5 = 4

Next multiply A and B for each skill

Pronunciation:
   3 × 2 = 6

Speaking:
   4 × 2 = 8

Writing:
   3 × 4 = 12

Put the skills in order, the one with the highest score first. That is the most important skill for you.

1. *Writing*
2. *Speaking*
3. *Pronunciation*

Step 4

As you can see on the next screen (Figure 4), the computer has done this for one student. The next step is to describe your exact difficulties with those skills and how you are going to improve them. In the example you can see a space where you can write down how many hours per week you will spend on that skill and when you want to reach your goal level. (In the next section there is more on setting goals.)

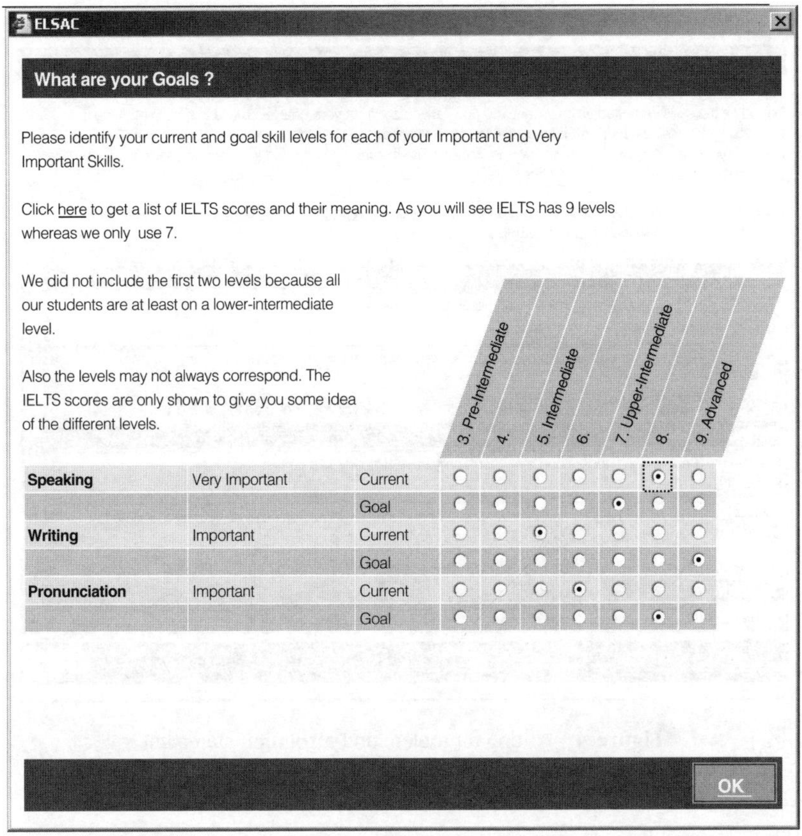

Figure 3 Choosing your current level and your goal level

Step 5

Start working! Look back at your notes regularly to see if you need to make any changes. Are you still spending the planned amount of time on the skills? Do you think your goal level needs to be changed? What about the date of reaching it? Have your specific problems changed? Have you found better ways to work on them?

A diagnostic test is just one way to find out about your English. Another way is by talking with other people, or by thinking about your IELTS score. Perhaps you did very well on listening but not so well on reading. However you found out about your English, you are now ready to do something about

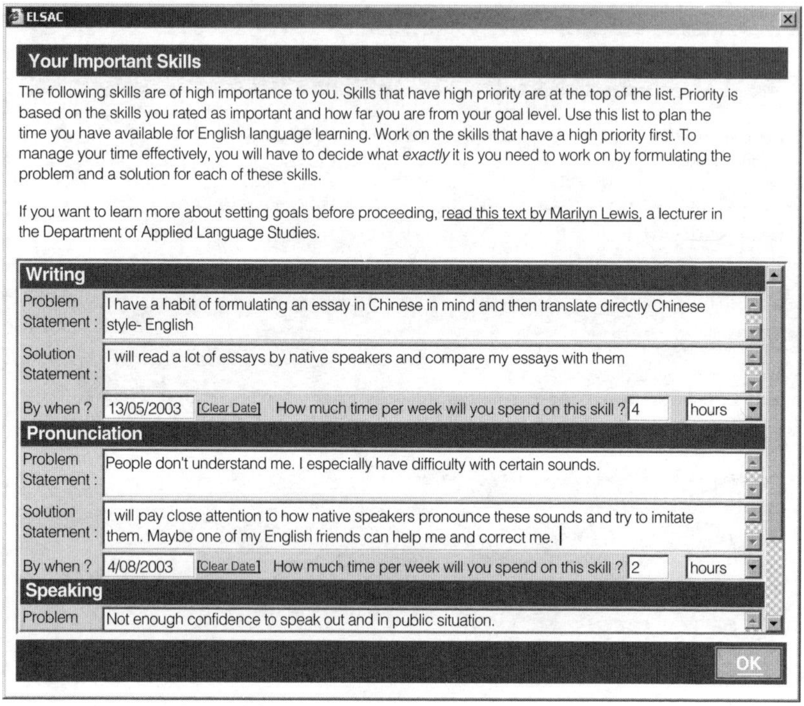

Figure 4   Writing a problem and a solution statement

it. The next part of the chapter gives you information about international English language tests.

▶ International English language tests: TOEFL and IELTS

What does the university want?

International students generally have to prove that their English is good enough to study at university. There are different ways to prove this but often students must either get a certain score on an English language test such as the TOEFL, IELTS or others, or ask to be exempt for some reason. An exemption means that you don't need to sit a test. The reason for the exemption can be that you have studied at high school in the country where you plan to go to university or that you have lived in an English-speaking country for a long time. Check with your university what their exemptions are.

Preparing for English language tests

The English language tests can be difficult and many students prepare for a long time by attending a special class or buying one of the many books which have copies of tests. You can take these language tests in your country or when you arrive in the new country.

The advantage of taking the test in the English-speaking country is that it will be easier for you to learn the language. Also, if you have joined a class you will be getting to know many other students with the same goals as you. On the other hand, if you take the test in the new country and fail, perhaps you will feel upset because you are far away from your family and friends. Many students who fail decide to study more and then sit the test again. You need to weigh up the advantages and disadvantages of taking the test in either place.

Let's look at the various tests and at ways of preparing for them.

TOEFL

TOEFL (Test of English as a Foreign Language) is an American language test that is widely recognised by universities around the world. There are two versions, a computer-based test and a paper-based test. It depends on where you take the test which version you will do.

How is TOEFL organised?

The paper test for TOEFL consists of two parts. In the first part there are tests of listening, structure, written expression, and reading comprehension. In the second part there is a Test of Written English (TWE). You cannot take the TWE separately but only as a part of the whole test, but you will receive a separate score for these two tests. Scores for the TOEFL test range from 310 to 677 and the scores for the TWE from 1 to 6. Each university has different requirements but a common score needed to be accepted at university is around 550 for the TOEFL and 4.5 for the TWE.

For the computer-based TOEFL test you get scores for the listening, structure and reading sections separately, ranging from 0 to 30 each. There is also a writing section with a score of 0–6. You receive a total score of between 0 and 300. Most universities require around 215. There may be a minimum score for the writing section. This is often 4.0.

There is also a test called the 'Test of Spoken English' or TSE, which measures your ability to communicate orally in English. It takes about twenty minutes. It is not part of the TOEFL test and you take it separately, but it was developed by the same people and usually you take it in the same place as the TOEFL test.

How and where can you take the TOEFL or TSE test?

For more information about how and where to take the test, check out the TOEFL websites.

---

www.toefl.org

You can also order materials to prepare for the test, such as CD roms, sample tests, etc. You can download sample questions and writing topics for free.

www.scoreitnow.org

'Score it now' is a service offered by a company that lets you practise writing and gives you scores for your essays. There is a fee for using this service.

Many other companies offer online resources, sometimes free and sometimes for a fee. Below we have listed two. There are also many books and CD roms to help you practise for the TOEFL test. Check with your local bookstore.

---

www.free-toefl.com/

www.freeesl.net/TOEFL/

IELTS

Another test that is recognised by many universities is IELTS (International English Language Testing System). It is not as widely accepted in the United States as the TOEFL test but is very common in Great Britain, Canada, Australia and New Zealand. The IELTS also has two versions which measure students' ability to study in English: an academic test for tertiary study and a general test for all other study and immigration purposes. Most universities require you to have a score for the academic test. IELTS is different from TOEFL in a number of ways but the main difference is that it contains a speaking part, unlike TOEFL (although you can sit a separate test for that, the TSE: see above).

You will get a score between 1 and 9 for all four parts as well as an overall score. Generally you will need 6.0 or higher for university entrance and often you cannot have a score lower than 5.5 on any of the four components. Some university departments or courses may ask for higher scores. For example, some schools of Medicine want you to have 8.5!

For more information, visit the IELTS homepage at:

www.ielts.org

Here you will find general information as well as some practice materials. As with TOEFL, there are many books, tapes and videos to help you prepare for IELTS.

How do the tests compare?
Table 1 compares the possible and required scores for the two tests.

Table 2 shows you what the various scores mean and how they compare between IELTS and TOEFL.

Cambridge certificates and other language tests
There are other, less widely used language tests such as the Cambridge examinations. These are at different levels and have a pass/fail score, unlike the TOEFL and IELTS. If you get a high enough score on the examination, you get a certificate. If you don't have that score, then you don't get a

Table 1   A comparison of the IELTS and the TOEFL tests

	Possible scores	University requirement
TOEFL (paper-based version)	310–677	550
TWE	1–6	4.5
TOEFL (computer-based version)	0–300	215
TOEFL (computer-based version) writing section	0–6	4.0
IELTS	1–9	6.0 (no band below 5.5)

Table 2 How do the tests compare? (Adapted from 'What is IELTS' – www.ielts.org/format.htm and LSE Language)

Description	IELTS	TOEFL (paper)	TOEFL (computer)
9.0 **Expert user** – Has fully operational command of the language: appropriate, accurate and fluent with complete understanding.	9.0	(700)	
8.0 **Very good user** – Has fully operational command of the language with only occasional unsystematic inaccuracies and inappropriacies. Misunderstandings may occur in unfamiliar situations. Handles complex detailed argumentation well.	8.0	650 647 643 640 637 633 630	280 277 273 270 267
7.0 **Good user** – Has operational command of the language, though with occasional inaccuracies, inappropriacies and misunderstandings in some situations. Generally handles complex language well and understands detailed reasoning.	7.0	627 623 620 617 613 610 607	263 260 257 253
	6.5	603 600 597 593 590 587 583 580 577 573 570 567 563 560 557 553	250 247 243 240 237 233 230 227 223 220 217
6.0 **Competent user** – Has generally effective command of the language despite some inaccuracies, inappropriacies and	6.0	550 547 543	213 210 206

TABLE 2 *Continued*

Description	IELTS	TOEFL (paper)	TOEFL (computer)
misunderstandings. Can use and understand		540	
fairly complex language, particularly in familiar		537	203
situations.		533	200
		530	197
		527	
		523	193
		520	190
		517	187
		513	183
		510	180
		507	
		503	177
	5.5	500	173
5.0 **Modest user** – Has partial command of the language, coping with overall meaning in most situations, though is likely to make many mistakes. Should be able to handle basic communication in own field.	5.0	450	133

certificate. In order of level from the easiest to the most difficult, here are some of these certificates:

- Cambridge FCE (First Certificate in English)
- CAE (Certificate in Advanced English)
- CPE (Certificate of Proficiency in English)

These three are used mainly in Great Britain and in other European coun-tries for university entrance.

On the following website you will find more information about these examinations:

www.cambridge-efl.org/exam

Placement tests and needs assessments

In addition to language tests that give a score for university entrance purposes, there are two other types of tests. A placement test will often be given by a language school when you first arrive, to decide what your level is. There are internationally used placement tests, such as the Quick Placement Test, but many schools develop their own. Usually you will not get a score for these tests.

A needs assessment is not a test. It is a way for your university or language school and for yourself to find out if you are likely to have any problems during your studies because of your English. Some universities ask students to do a needs assessment even if they already have an IELTS or TOEFL score. Again, you will generally not be given a score but if the needs assessment indicates that there are areas of your English that need improving, you may be directed to a language course or other support.

2 Planning your Studies

In Chapter 1 we discussed decisions you had to make before leaving your country. This chapter is for students who have already chosen their university and now need to plan the details of their programme. The first part is for undergraduates (people studying for a first degree) and talks about choosing your major and minor subjects. The second part of the chapter, which is for graduates, explains the meaning of various names and programmes.

This chapter answers the following questions:

* What words are used to describe parts of a degree?
* What are a student's choices in planning a first degree?
* What are postgraduate studies?
* How do students actually enrol at university?

▶ Planning your undergraduate degree

What is a degree programme?

Your undergraduate degree programme includes all the subjects you study for one qualification such as a BA or a BSc. Degree programmes are usually organised into courses. Thus a science degree (BSc) could include courses in Computer Science, Chemistry, Geology etc., while an arts degree (BA) has courses in English, History, Chinese, Sociology etc. Most universities allow students to take courses in more than one faculty (such as the Science Faculty, the Commerce Faculty or the Arts Faculty), but for other specialist degrees that lead to one particular profession you may need to study all your subjects in just one faculty.

Degrees usually take three or four years to complete, but students who take two different areas of study for a conjoint degree, such as a BA or BSc, could take five years to complete their studies. A conjoint (or combined) degree means taking some subjects from each of two degrees, instead of taking six years to finish two separate degrees.

There are two main systems for degrees in English-speaking countries. Some countries, such as Canada, follow the United States system, while others such as Australia, New Zealand and South Africa, follow the British system.

The American degree system

In the United States, degree programmes usually take four years. In the first year students usually study general education subjects (like maths, natural sciences, English) and at the end of the year they decide what they will major in. Then, for the next three years, they take courses in their major. Even students who already know what they want to graduate in take the general education subjects in the first year, although they can start taking specific subjects for their major at the same time.

The British degree system

In the British system, degree programmes are organised like a triangle. For example, Figure 5 explains how a BA (Bachelor of Arts degree) moves from the first to the third year.

Major subjects

Your major subject is the one (or sometimes more than one) which you study for longest. If you plan to study Engineering then you would enrol for a BE

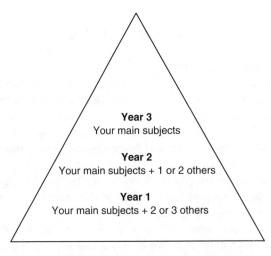

Year 3
Your main subjects

Year 2
Your main subjects + 1 or 2 others

Year 1
Your main subjects + 2 or 3 others

Figure 5 British degree structure

(a Bachelor of Engineering degree) and take courses in one of the following: civil engineering, electrical engineering or mechanical engineering. If most of your courses are in civil engineering then that is called your major and your degree will be a BE (civil). You normally study your major for all three years of the degree.

Minor subjects

You study minor subjects for less time than your major subjects and you don't take as many of them. If, for example, you were studying for a major in Geography you could still study English for one or two semesters. English would be your minor subject. Generally the courses you take for a minor are all related to one subject (such as English or Biology), although minors can be taken in other departments and even in other faculties. Of course you need to enrol formally for a subject whether it is a minor or a major, otherwise it may not be added to your academic records. When you enrol at the start of the semester the enrolment person will check that your department will accept the minor you want to do. (See Chapter 1 for more on enrolling.)

Can students choose any subjects?

There is some freedom in planning a degree but there are also some restrictions. When you are planning your degree you need to know the difference between courses you *must* take and courses you *may* take. You also need to know which subjects must be studied before others.

Prerequisites

A prerequisite is a course you MUST study before you can do another course. For example a prerequisite for studying *Syntax and Semantics* could be a pass in *Introduction to Linguistics*.

Exemptions

Sometimes students needn't take the prerequisite because they have taken the subject before or are very good at it. Then the department will say 'You can have an exemption,' or 'You are exempt from doing French 101 because you have studied in France for a year. You may go straight to French 201.'

Electives

Most studies have a number of electives (or optional subjects). These are subjects that you are free to choose and that don't have to be related to your major. For example, you might want to major in Geography but study Spanish for one year.

▶ **Planning your postgraduate programme**

So far in this chapter we have talked about students who are beginning an undergraduate degree such as a BA, a BSc, or a BCom. Many international students are actually postgraduates. In other words they already have a first degree and are now enrolling for one of these:

- a Master's degree;
- a postgraduate diploma;
- a doctorate.

The rest of this chapter has extra information for these people.

Postgraduate or graduate?
Students who already have a degree and are now enrolling for another one, are called postgraduate students or graduate students. Different countries (and sometimes different universities) use one or another of these terms:

- a graduate or postgraduate student;
- a graduate or postgraduate course;
- graduate or postgraduate studies.

You will soon find out which term is used at your university. Let's just say that (post)graduate students are the people who 'take a higher degree' or 'do graduate study'. We use both terms in this chapter. Here are some examples of postgraduate degrees:

- a graduate diploma in Business Studies;
- a Master's degree in Biology;
- a PhD (Doctor of Philosophy), EdD (Doctor of Education), MD (Doctor of Medicine), DocFA (Doctor of Fine Arts) etc.

These are just examples. There are others.

What is a postgraduate programme?
For postgraduate studies, traditions differ from place to place. In American universities any Master's degree or PhD includes some taught courses. This means that you would be sitting in classes, as you did when you were an undergraduate, except that the classes would probably be smaller. However, in universities th
at follow the British tradition your entire PhD may be made up of your own original work, which you do with the guidance of a supervisor. Table 3 summarises three types of postgraduate degree.

The words *thesis* and *dissertation* are used for the original work that a student does with supervision from a staff member.

Table 3 Types of postgraduate study

Name	Details	Who can take it?
A postgraduate diploma	Usually one year Usually courses + a research project	Usually people with a first degree Work experience may count
A Master's degree	One or two years A dissertation or thesis	People with good grades
A doctorate (PhD)	Several years May include course work	People with high grades

Planning your programme

As a postgraduate student you have choices to make about the programme you choose and about the subjects in that programme. There are three ways of making up your mind about which choice to make.

1. Look on the website or in the Departmental Handbook and read their descriptions of the different choices. Ask yourself questions like these:

    •   Do I want to know more about topics I am already interested in?
    •   Is there some new topic I want to start learning about?
    •   Is there a 'famous person' in this department whose lectures I would like to attend?

2. Visit the person who has the job of advising students. Most departments have a graduate adviser who will spend time with you after you arrive at the university. Sometimes the results of your first university degree suggest that one choice or another is better for you.

3. Talk to students who have already started the course. Ask questions like these:

    •   Which choice did you make and why?
    •   How did you decide? Who helped you to decide?
    •   Are you happy with your choice?

Course work or thesis?

When you enrol for a postgraduate degree such as an MA or an MSc your only choice may be between:

- taught courses only; OR
- thesis only; OR
- courses plus a thesis.

In taught courses you attend lectures (and maybe tutorials), you do assignments and you may also take a final examination. Some students choose to do courses because they have come a long way to learn from people who are famous in their subjects.

▶ Enrolling in a university

Enrolling takes time but it isn't difficult. In this section you will see what information you need to have ready when you start to apply. As you will see, there are differences depending on your present qualifications and perhaps on your country of origin.

Who can enrol?
After you have decided on your university, it is time to apply for admission. Universities have different criteria (rules) that decide if you are eligible (allowed to study for a course).

Previous qualifications
Some universities ask you to prove only that you have completed your high school studies. Others want a high GPA, or Grade Point Average, which is the average score you received in (usually) your last year at high school. Many universities accept international secondary school qualifications such as the International Baccalaureat.

If you are still at secondary school you could ask your school for more information, or see:

  http://www.ibo.org.

Between some countries there are agreements about high school qualifications. For example, if you have spent time in a New Zealand high school and want to study in Great Britain, your New Zealand high school diploma is recognised by British universities.

Here is one example of a requirement:

To study in this department at this university you must:

- have a high school diploma, a public examination score etc.;
- have previous experience in studying that subject;
- be proficient [good] enough in the English language to study in English.

(See the information in this chapter on the IELTS and TOEFL qualifications.)

As well as the general criteria for entering a particular university, some faculties also have their own entry requirements. For example, to study Medicine you generally need to have a very good GPA, which means your course results. The best thing to do is to enquire at the faculty where you want to study, or look on their website.

If your qualifications are not recognised or are not high enough, there are three things you can do:

- You can go back to school in the new country to try for a higher examination score.
- You can enrol in a Foundation Studies programme. Many universities offer these courses in language and academic subjects to prepare international and other students for university.
- You can apply for provisional entrance, which is usually given only to students who:

  (a) don't have the required qualifications, BUT
  (b) have always received good scores in school or perhaps in another university.

Exchange arrangements

As we mentioned before, some countries or universities have a special relationship with other countries or universities, making it easier for students to study overseas. Sometimes this is done as part of an exchange programme where students go from one country to another and the same number go the other way. In this case one of the countries may help pay the university fees or travel expenses.

Enrolling for postgraduate courses

If you are applying for postgraduate study then you must meet extra requirements. For a Master's degree you normally have to have a Bachelor's degree in the same subjects and a higher than average GPA (Grade Point Average). Requirements for postgraduate diplomas are usually similar to those for a Master's. If you want to do a Master's degree or graduate diploma in a subject different from your undergraduate studies you may have to enrol for a bridging programme. This will be made up of courses recommended by your graduate advisor.

Applying for a doctorate is a bit more complicated. Generally, before you can be accepted you need to:

- have research experience (e.g. you must have completed a Master's degree, written a thesis, or worked in research);
- be successful in your studies (e.g. have a high GPA);
- write a proposal.

In Chapter 2 you can read more about postgraduate studies.

Finding the right papers

If you know, or think, that you are eligible to study at a particular university, then the next step is to collect all your papers (documents) and send them in to prove that you meet the criteria. Both local and international students need to do this. Here are three things to remember about the documents.

1. All the documents need to be either originals or certified copies, which means that the copies are signed by someone such as a lawyer or a Justice of the Peace (JP). You can find someone to sign in one of these ways:

   - Ask at the enrolment offices for a Justice of the Peace. (A staff member may be able to do this.)
   - Look in the phone book or at the city council offices for a Justice of the Peace.

2. If your qualifications or other documents are not in English you usually have to get them translated by an official translator. You cannot simply translate them yourself or ask a friend to do it. Some universities can help with this. However, universities which have many students from the same country may accept documents in your language. For example, many European universities allow documents in English, French, German and other national languages, while universities with large numbers of Chinese students sometimes allow documents in that language.

3. When showing your qualifications you often need to send transcripts (records of your grades at high school or at another university) to show which subjects you have taken and the scores you got for them.

Table 4 Are you ready?

Do I have . . . ?	What if I don't?
Good English proficiency	Take English courses.
Proof of my English proficiency (test results)	Sit an English test such as TOEFL or IELTS.
A visa	Apply for a visa from the nearest Embassy or High Commission of the country where you plan to study.
A sufficient GPA	Choose a different university or a different course of study with lower requirements.
Certified copies of my diplomas	Have your copies certified by a lawyer, or a Justice of the Peace.
Translations of diplomas etc.	Have the diplomas professionally translated.
Transcripts of grades	Ask your high school or your last university.

Checklist for enrolling

Once you have collected all your papers, the next step is to fill in the enrolment forms. Enrolment in most English-speaking countries is done either by filling in application forms by hand and posting them, or by enrolling online on the university's website. If you are enrolling online there is usually email support available. Use the checklist in Table 4 to make sure you have everything ready.

3 Improving your English

In the first chapter we discussed ways of finding out about your English level and then in Chapter 2 we talked about planning your degree studies. Whether you have already enrolled or whether you are still preparing for that stage, as a second-language speaker of English you will also want to go on improving your proficiency in English.

The answer to the question 'How can I go on improving my English?' is different for everyone. Some students find that although they know a lot about English grammar it is difficult to use it when talking and writing. Others know the language of their subject area (e.g. science, computing, business) fairly well but find everyday language difficult. Still others can read the technical language but don't recognise it spoken in lectures.

This chapter answers the following questions:

- How can I plan to improve my English?
- Do universities offer English courses for new speakers of English?
- How can I improve my word level?

▶ Setting language learning goals

Finding out your level and setting goals are closely linked. That is why we started talking about goals at the same time as showing how to do a Needs Analysis. In this section you find out more about setting goals for yourself.

What are language learning goals?
Goals are statements that say what you want to learn. For example:

I want to understand the lecturers when they talk fast.

My goal is to be a better essay writer.

Goals help people understand why they are learning a language in a particular way and what they hope to be able to do at the end. Goals may relate to language skills. What kinds of speaking do you need to practise? Maybe you can speak in conversations with friends but find it difficult to do class presentations. Maybe your listening skills are quite good when you are watching TV but you find it difficult to understand native speakers when they talk to you at normal speaking speed.

Why set goals?

There are many reasons why students find goals helpful. For one thing, goals are a way of being in charge of your learning. Instead of just going to a class and hoping that the teacher will do a good job, you think about what and how you are learning. Goals are also important as a way of helping you organise your time. You don't want to spend time in a general English course if your main goal is to learn to write. Here is one student's goal for organising her time.

> *I plan to spend two evenings a week in a class and another four hours study-ing on my own between classes.*

A third reason for setting goals is that they help you to be definite rather than vague. Instead of saying just 'I want to learn English', you might say 'I want to learn 2,000 new words by. . . .' To set more definite goals, think about the times when you have problems. Is writing difficult only when you haven't got enough time? Is speaking difficult only in formal settings such as during lectures? See how precise these two students were about their problems.

Student 1

> *I thought I was quite good at writing but when I started studying at university, lecturers often asked us to summarise chapters from the course book. I found this very difficult. My summaries were much too sub-jective. It took me quite some time to realise that academic writing is very different from normal writing.*

Student 2

> *After I arrived in Glasgow (Scotland) at first I couldn't understand anything of what people were saying. At school we had been taught American English but not other dialects. Listening to lectures was easier because I knew most of the academic vocabulary, but speaking to people on the street was a nightmare. After I studied the differences in pronunciation between Scottish English and American English and learned some common expressions it was easier.*

If you can name your exact difficulty, you can work on that. Let's see how you can move from naming your problem to setting your goals.

How do students decide their goals?

Students we asked talked about three main ways of deciding on good goals: ask senior students; do a quick needs analysis; or take a test.

One common way of deciding goals is to talk with students who have already gone overseas to study. Here is one answer.

Lecturers won't tell you exactly what to write in essays. You have to find out for yourself.

The answer led the student to set this goal:

I want to find out what makes a good essay in the subjects I'm studying.

Another senior student said:

I hope you can read fast because there is plenty of reading to do at university.

As a result the student wrote:

I plan to find a short course on how to read fast and still understand what I read.

Another way is to do a quick needs analysis. In Chapter 1 we saw how to do a computer-based needs analysis. Even without this you could ask and answer your own questions. Here are four examples.

1. *Can I understand many different accents?*

   It's not enough to understand just the accent of the country because, as we have seen, university lecturers come from all countries of the world and have many different English accents. Try listening to radio talks from many different countries of the world.

2. *Can I talk freely to native speakers who speak at normal speed?*

   If your answer is 'No', try joining a university club so you can meet English speakers while you are doing something interesting.

3. *Do I know the vocabulary of my area of study (e.g. words related to business or science)?*

    If the answer to this question is 'not well enough', look in the university bookshop for an 'introduction to . . .' book in your subject.

4. *Can I write about essay topics once I understand them?*

    If writing essays is the problem, see Chapter 8 on how to improve your writing. Now let's look in more detail on how to reach your goals.

▶ **Pre-university English courses**

Finding out about courses

Even before you leave your country there are ways of improving your English. Most countries now have many classes where English is taught. There are probably some that teach general English at schools near you, but check with universities and colleges about academic English courses that prepare you for university study. Great Britain, for example, has British Councils in many countries around the world which offer courses and advice for students intending to visit or study in Great Britain. Other countries such as Australia and the USA have similar arrangements. Many embassies can also offer help. Try these websites.

For information about the British Council and a list of offices around the world, check their website:

www.britishcouncil.org/where/index.htm

This site lists over 6000 language courses in 90 countries!

www.language-learning.net

On this site you can search by country:

www.esldirectory.com

Another useful site is:

www.onestopenglish.com

Deciding what is the right course

Some of the courses may not give you what you want. Perhaps they do not prepare you especially for the English used in the country you are going to or the kind of English you will need for your studies. How do you know a certain course is right for you? There are several things to pay attention to, such as the quality of the course, the level, its contents, the price, class times and the length of the course. Let's look at these in detail now.

The quality of the course

It is hard to find out beforehand whether a course is good or not. If possible, talk to people who have been to the course and ask about their experiences. Read information about the various courses schools offer. Check their websites if they have one, or call them if they don't and ask them to send you a brochure. Does their programme look interesting? Does it cover what you want to learn? Do their teachers have good qualifications? Does the school have a good 'name'? Is it a private school or is it linked to a larger institution such as a university? Do they have good facilities (computers, self-access centre, library etc.)? Do they organise activities such as excursions? Are most of the students from the same country or are there students from all around the world? What is the average size of the classes?

When you enrol for the course, ask whether you need to pay for the whole course at the start. If not, you can leave if you are not pleased.

Content and level of the course

It is important to make sure that the course is suitable for your level. Are there enough classes to be sure you will be in a class that is right for you? Some smaller language schools don't have enough students to organise classes at many levels. That is not to say that smaller language schools are not good. Sometimes they have fewer people in one class. You need to ask yourself whether the course covers all the skills you need to work on.

If you are preparing to go to university you may want to choose a course that focuses on academic English and teaches skills such as notetaking, listening to lectures, writing essays etc. If you have difficulty in speaking and understanding the local accent, then you should choose a course that spends a lot of time on these skills. Some schools can offer courses for Business English or English for other study/work areas. It is always a good idea to have a look at the course book. Have a look at the last pages to see what the goal level of the course is.

Length of the course and class times

It is important that the times of the course suit your schedule. If you are working or studying at the same time you need to make sure that you have enough time to go to class. Check to see how many hours per week you will have classes and at what times. If it is important for you to study in the morning or in the evening then make sure to ask to be scheduled into these classes when enrolling for a course.

Also check the course finish date. Does the course finish before your university study starts? If not, it may be better to enrol for a shorter course. Sometimes for visa purposes you are required to study a minimum number of hours per week, such as 25 hours. You should check this with the Immigration Office. This may limit your choice. If you don't want to be bound to certain class times then a distance course on the Internet may be more suitable for you. Be sure to check whether you must be online at specific times or if you can log on at any time.

Course fees
Finally, the price of a course is also important. You have to ask yourself if you think the course is worth it. If you can't afford a course then you can always try one of the other ways of studying English mentioned in this chapter. Some courses offer you a certificate that may be recognised by the university or employers. In that case that may be an extra argument for taking the course.

▶ Other ways of improving your English

Some students don't have time or money to go to language courses. Others feel that there are other, better ways of learning. Below we list some examples.

Learn one-to-one from a native speaker
Some people prefer to learn one-to-one from a native English speaker, even if that person is not a teacher. This method suits people who already have quite good English but want to improve their standard. It is particularly helpful if you want to get used to different accents. Remember, though, that at university your lecturers will not all be from the country where you are studying. Most universities today have staff from all over the world.

If there are many overseas people working in your city you could put up a note on the notice boards of international companies asking for people from the country that you are going to. Other good places to put up notices are embassies and clubs of people from overseas who work in your country. If you find someone who wants to learn your language then you can help each other by doing a language exchange; you could first practise the language you want to learn (English), and next the language the other person wants to learn (Korean, Chinese etc.).

Learning one-to-one means you can ask questions any time you like without stopping the class. Don't be surprised, though, if your teacher cannot answer grammar questions about the English language. A person with a degree in Engineering or Medicine, say, may not understand when you ask about the past conditional tense. As you probably know in your own language, there is a difference between being a language user and being able to describe the language. On the other hand the person you find may be able to answer your questions about living in a particular city or country.

Use the media or websites

If you can't find anyone to talk to, you can at least listen to English. On the Internet there are thousands of sites where you can listen to English radio, watch the news, hear the sports results etc. By reading newspapers from the country you are going to, you can get used to expressions/vocabulary that are used there and learn about its culture. You can search for websites by country or even region and in that way you can listen to the accent you want.

> For a list of newspapers and audio and video broadcasts on the Internet, look on:
>
> dir.yahoo.com/News_and_Media
>
> You can search by country, region or city.

Online courses

If you prefer to study in a more organised way then you can enrol in an online language course (on the Internet). There are now some very good language schools on the Internet. If you do find lessons that cover your own level and interests, an advantage of Internet courses is that you can study when and where you want, including in your own home.

Usually you pay for these courses but often they are far cheaper than a 'real' course and many websites even offer free English lessons. Make sure that you have the right equipment (computer, headphones, microphone, Internet access) to take part in the course and that you know what extra costs there are, such as books and CD roms that you may need to buy.

Check out this website for a list of online English courses:

www.eslcafe.com/search/Online_English_Courses

Two very good ones are:

www.englishtown.com

and

www.bellenglish.com

If you want to improve your English for one study area like Business or Medicine, then these courses may be too general. In that case there are some good books on the market that you can use for self-study. If you can't order these through your local bookshop then some of the publishers let you buy their books through the Internet, using a credit card.

Check out this website for lists of English-language learning materials:

www.eslcafe.com/bookstore

So, to summarise, before you go overseas you can:

* enrol in an English course;
* find a native speaker of the country you are going to;
* listen to audio and video recordings on the Internet;
* read online newspapers from the new country/region;
* enrol in online English courses;
* use self-study English language learning materials.

▶ Improving your English in the new country

After you arrive in the new country it will be easier to improve your English as you have many more opportunities to use the language. Below are some ideas and suggestions.

Use English in the new community

Especially in the beginning when you have just arrived in the new country it is important to go out and speak to as many people as you can to get used to the accent. Listen to local radio stations; watch the news and TV programmes; read local newspapers; join a sports club.

Try to make friends with the locals. When you come back home you can speak Chinese or Korean with your own friends again! One great way to force yourself to speak English and to learn about the culture of the country is through a homestay (you can read more about homestays in Chapter 11). You live with a family of native speakers and share meals and sometimes go out and do things together.

People sometimes say to English language learners, 'Whatever you do, do it in English!' However, we all need to be able to talk about serious things with someone who understands us. You don't have to cut yourself off from everyone who speaks your own language. Other students from your country can be a great support.

General English language courses

Some students take English courses when they arrive in the new country. This is a good idea because the teachers in the course are probably from that country and therefore you can learn the local accent. However, because it's likely that many of the students in your class will be from your country or from similar cultural backgrounds, it is easy to make friends with them.

To find courses in the new country you can search the Internet. If possible use a search engine specific to the country you are going to. Altavista and Yahoo have many country-specific search engines. Other places to search for courses are Tourist Information Centres and libraries.

For example, if you want to study in Auckland, New Zealand, you go to:

> www.altavista.co.nz

and type the following:

> 'English course' AND 'Auckland'

You should then see a list of English schools in Auckland.

▶ University credit courses in English

So far all the ideas for learning English in the new country have been outside the university. Universities, too, will have courses that may suit you, either as part of your degree or as an extra.

University English language credit courses
Some universities offer English courses for credits, which means that you can gain points for your degree. This allows you to work on your English in study time.

What can you expect from a credit course?
Sometimes individual faculties offer English language courses that focus specifically on the English you need for that study area. It goes without saying that these can be very useful. If you are studying for a BCom (Bachelor of Commerce), for example, find out how many English language courses you are allowed to take in that degree. Here is an example from one university:

> 'Your degree programme is made up of 14 points. You must take at least __ of these points within the Commerce Department. If you want to, you may take __ points in any other department of this university.'

These courses often focus on academic English. They help you to acquire the skills you need for successful university study, such as listening to lectures, notetaking, giving presentations etc. Some students find that taking an English language credit course helps them with their other studies and also adds points to their main degree.

How are English credit courses organised?
English credit courses may be offered at different levels like this:

  100 level = a first-year course
  200 level = a second-year course
  300 level = a third-year course

Usually students start at the 100 level and work up to higher levels. However, if someone's level of English is too good for the first-year course they can sometimes do one of the higher courses immediately.

English credit courses are often specialised. Here are some examples of titles of courses for learning to write at university:

- ESOL courses for University Writing;
- Academic Writing;
- Essay Writing;
- Advanced Academic Written English.

As well as writing courses, you may find courses for other skills: speaking, listening and reading. All these courses are for students whose English is already good enough for university study but who want to make their English even better.

How can I find out about these courses?
The main places for finding out about courses are:

1. the department's website;
2. the department's handbook;
3. talking with the teachers.

The department which teaches these courses will have different names in different universities. Here are some examples:

- English Language Centre
- Language Academy
- Language School
- Department of Applied Linguistics
- Language Institute

Now let's see what one university English course looks like.

One university writing course
The content of the course and the way you are assessed (tested) changes from place to place, but here is one example of a course description from one university.

ENGWRIT 101 ENGLISH WRITING FOR ACADEMIC PURPOSES

This course is useful to all first-year students unfamiliar with academic work, to good students who wish to expand their repertoire for writing strategies and improve their skills, and to students with writing difficulties. The course will help students develop efficient and effective techniques for generating, organising, drafting and editing texts.

It also involves the analysis of various kinds of academic writing. Topics include the structure of argumentative essays, essays of comparison and contrast, descriptive writing, reviews and problem solution texts. The structure of essays in different academic fields will also be discussed.

Summer School, Semester One or Semester Two, City Campus
Lecture times:

Summer School: Monday and Tuesday 10–12
Semester One: Monday and Wednesday 10–11
Semester Two: Monday and Wednesday 10–12

Because some of the activities were very different from the ways students had learned in their own country, at the end of the course the teacher asked what they thought about some of these activities. Their responses are shown with each activity.

Peer teaching in a writing course
This is how peer teaching was organised.

Peer teaching

1. Work in five small groups. Each group reads and discusses one section of pages ___ of the course book. [*5 ways to expand a topic sentence into a paragraph*]
2. Discuss these questions:

   (a) What exactly is this method of expanding the topic sentence?
   (b) What sort of topics could be expanded in this way?
   (c) What sort of words and phrases join ideas that are linked in this way?

3. Plan an interesting way to teach the content to the rest of the class.
4. Each group then teaches their section to the whole class.

What did the students think about peer teaching?

Teaching others leads to teaching oneself. If you don't understand you can't explain it to others.

Students know which part they don't understand.

Everyone participates.

Journal writing

Each week students wrote to their teacher about how they were getting along with their writing. They might write questions:

How can I write better introductions?

Or they might express their feelings:

The most difficult part of essay writing for me is . . .

The teacher then wrote back individual answers.
At the end of the course two students had this to say about journal writing:

It is a good way to build confidence with writing . . .

The teacher can know how much I understand of the lesson.

Peer feedback

From time to time when the class had written a paragraph or even a whole essay, the teacher asked students to change papers and write comments on one another's work. Sometimes the teacher suggested what to write.

What did you think about the ideas in this paragraph?

Do you have any suggestions for putting paragraphs in a better order?

Mark sentences where the meaning is not quite clear.

Although at first the students found it a strange idea to have their peers make comments on their writing, by the end of the course, this is what they said about it.

The others sometimes notice something you don't realise.

Feedback from students can help to establish social relations with each other.

Group interviews

As part of their learning to write, students interviewed one another about the way they could learn to be better writers.

Students can share their experiences, their stories of success and failure.

One can always learn from others' experiences.

It improves social skills.

Question time

In one lesson the teacher said she would teach for an hour only, to answer students' questions. They had five minutes at first to write down their questions and then each one was answered slowly and carefully with examples. Each student had to ask one question. Here is what the students thought about Question Time.

Students will be interested to get their answers in class.

Students who are usually too shy for asking questions are forced to do so (even if this might be negative in the first place) and therefore might get used to questions in general.

All students have to talk, even shy ones.

Summary of activities in university credit courses

We have seen the activities in just one academic writing class. Other classes will have other types of activity. In general, though, teachers plan the class activities for many reasons. Here are some of them.

To help students understand better

When teachers explain things they may think you know more than you do. When students explain things to one another, then they may make things clearer.

To show students new ways of learning

People learn in different ways. Some people think the way they learn is the very best way and they may be right, but until you hear about other ways you can't be sure. If you have 15 people in your writing class there could be 15 new and useful ideas for you to hear about.

To make learning more enjoyable

Sitting in rows looking at the teacher at the front is only one way of learning. When you talk with other students about what you are learning, the classes can be more enjoyable and varied.

To encourage everyone to take part
Another problem about sitting in rows is that it's easy for your mind to wander. When you are working in twos and threes everyone has to think and work.

To make students independent learners
If you rely on the teacher to tell you exactly what to do and how, then it's harder when you come to write essays out of class. If you learn to work with others, you can always form study groups with people you know.

▶ Self-access centres

A self-access centre (SAC) or an independent learning centre (ILC) is a place where students come to work on their English by themselves. Many universities nowadays have SACs and so do many language schools. These SACs have books, cassettes, videos and computer programmes for students to work with. Many SACs also organise language learning activities where students work in pairs or small groups. Usually staff are available to help students with their learning.

> Self-access centres are sometimes called different names such as 'independent learning centre', 'language learning centre' or 'self-study centre'. Also used are their abbreviations: SAC, ILC, LLC. We will use SAC here.

SACs can be a good way to improve your English. They have a number of advantages over language courses:

- You can come and study there when it suits you, unlike language classes that are at fixed times. Many SACs are open in the evenings and at weekends.
- You can work with materials that are right for your needs and interests. If you study, say, Commerce or Engineering, then in the SAC you can find materials to help you learn English for those topics. In general language courses these are not always covered.
- You can work at your own pace and your own level of difficulty. Also, you can choose how much time to spend on a skill.

- SACs help you improve your skills in working by yourself. This is especially helpful when you study at university.

Students' comments

Because learning by yourself is not always easy, many SACs help students in various ways to do this. Read the following ideas from students.

- *I went to an introductory session that the SAC organises twice per week. That showed me what materials there are and how I can use them. I also found out about the activities the SAC organises. There is a discussion group, a movie club, a reading club, writing seminars and conversation practice. I found the discussion group very useful because it helped me lose my fear of speaking in public.*

- *In our SAC language teachers are usually there to help us. I found them very helpful. They have shown me how to study by myself and how to choose the right materials.*

- *I signed up for a weekly 'Language Advisory Session'. You sit down with a teacher and talk about your learning. I found it very useful and got a lot of advice on what to study and how. It also helped me to study hard as we set goals for the next session. I felt more comfortable about studying by myself as the teacher told me when I was doing well and when I wasn't.*

- *There are many books in our SAC about how to study by yourself. One of our teachers has also prepared a small booklet with strategies for self-study. I use these books to find tips on how to best study vocabulary or to choose the right materials.*

- *I found out that the SAC has many materials to practise writing. Writing every day has helped me to really improve my English.*

One of the students mentioned that some of the books she used in the SAC taught her strategies for studying by herself. Here is one such book that you can use yourself:

Ellis, G., and B. Sinclair (2000) *Learning to Learn English: A Course in Learner Training* (Cambridge: Cambridge University Press).

Materials and activities in the SAC

You need to decide which of the many materials and activities in the Centre suit you best. Most SACs have a catalogue that helps you to find resources. Although there are many different ways in which SACs organise their materials, usually you can search by skill and subskill. In Figure 6, you will find an example of a computer-based catalogue. You can search by title, which is useful if you know the book or tape you are looking for. If the name of the book is *English for Meetings* then search for 'Meetings'. If you type in 'English' then of course you will find too many titles.

In the example shown in Figure 6 you can also search by difficulty level. If you are not sure about your level then try some of the materials to find out what level suits you. If you have taken a needs analysis, you will have a pretty good idea of what skills and subskills you need to work on. In Figure 6 you can see that you can choose from 'listening', 'reading', and 'writing' etc. For each one there are also a number of subskills. In this example you can see the subskills for 'writing'. If you don't know which subskills to work on then just search for the main skill. Some catalogues also let you search for particular accents (as in this example, under 'pronunciation') or particular situations, etc. If all this sounds difficult,

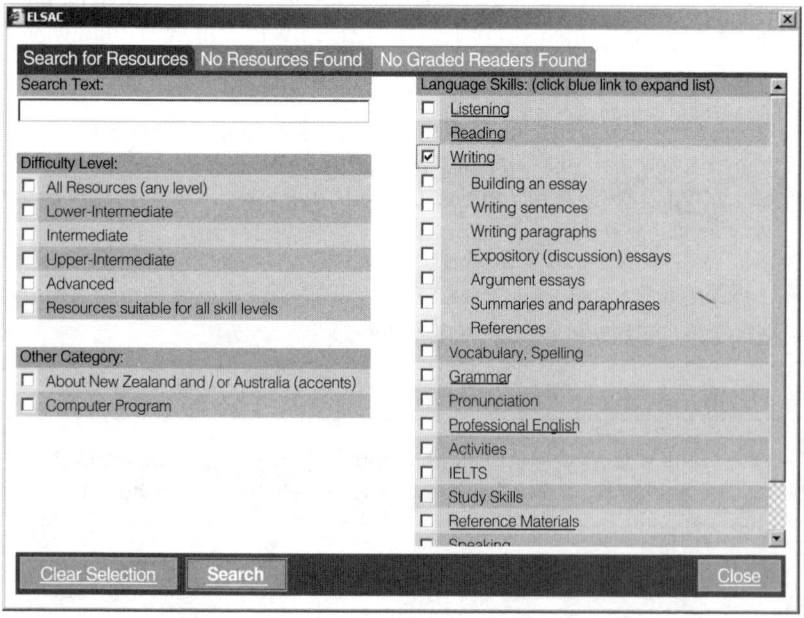

Figure 6 Searching for materials

don't worry. Usually there are instructions in the SAC on how to use the catalogue.

Learning journals

We saw that students in a writing class kept learning journals, but you can also keep one by yourself. Many SACs have a Learning Record or Portfolio that lets you write down which materials you have worked with and what you have learned. By thinking about what you have learned you can see improvements and decide what to do next time. Look at this example of one learner's learning journal (Table 5) where she looks at what she has done the last week.

Language conversation exchange

We saw earlier in the chapter that people in your own country could be interested in learning from you as well as teaching you. The same system can

Table 5   Example of a learning journal

Week	Skill	How did I work on this skill?
27	SPEAKING IN PUBLIC	I went to a conversation class in the SAC
	Comments	I now feel more confident to speak but I noticed that people find it difficult to understand my pronunciation. I will have to work on this.
	Plan for next week	I will start doing a language exchange with an English student who wants to learn Chinese. I will also find some materials in the SAC that will help me to improve my pronunciation.
27	WRITING SUMMARIES	I used the book that my teacher showed me. Also my Science teacher gave me some summaries from good students.
	Comments	I can see the differences between my writing and a native speaker's but it's difficult to write like them. I will need more practice.
	Plan for next week	I will continue to use the book and ask a native speaker to read my summaries and to give me feedback.

work at your university if they have language exchange programmes, or conversation exchange programmes. These are organised by the self-access centre, or the International Office, the Student Learning Centre or outside the university in community centres or libraries.

Language exchange programmes match learners of one language with learners of another language. In each case one person is a native speaker of the language the other person wants to learn. So, for example, if you are a native speaker of Korean then you can do an exchange with a native speaker of English who wants to learn your language. This is a great way to practise speaking and it's free!

The student learning centre/study skills centre

Most universities have a Student Learning Centre (SLC), Study Skills Centre or Learning Support Centre which help students with the skills they need to be successful in their university study. Many offer short courses on topics such as 'Organising your Learning', 'How to Plan your Thesis' etc. Usually there is also a room with books and information about study skills, examples of essays etc. In some universities the SAC and the SLC are the same.

▶ Learning new words

It's easy to think: 'There are so many new words to learn at university. How can I understand them all?' We cannot go through all your subject language here, although we can show you ways of understanding it. If you have already started your study, then try this before you read the rest of the chapter. Think of some new words you have heard or read in your university study. Write them down. Then, as you read this chapter, see if any of the ideas here help you with understanding the new words on your list.

General suggestions

Some students start by trying to learn all the new words they meet. That is a very difficult task. You need to have a plan for choosing the words (and ideas) to learn. Here are some suggestions.

1. Learn the words you hear and read many times.
2. Some words you need to learn to help you when you read and hear them. Other words are worth learning so that you can say and write them.
3. Learn words in their context phrases rather than by themselves.
4. Don't waste too much time on translating all the words into your own language. Translation helps only if you have already studied this subject

at university in your country and you already know the specialised word in your own language.

Subject words

One place to start learning new words is in the language of your own subjects. Let's talk about two subject areas as examples: Mathematics and Law.

Mathematical language

Mathematical language is special because it is very precise. It uses a special language to describe numbers, and symbols such as $\sqrt{}$, ∞, %. As well as its words, the type of sentence used in mathematics texts is less varied than in other subjects. It is often not necessary to use past tenses, or pronouns except 'it' etc. Instead, maths texts make many statements. That is, they say that something is such and such and then they provide proof of that.

Legal language

Law is another area of study that has its own language. Apart from many technical words, there are also words from general English which are used in specific ways that have little meaning outside the field of law.

Law texts generally have much longer sentences than texts in other fields and there are many statements and very few questions. This is logical because law texts are usually prescriptive, meaning that they tell people what to do and what not to do. Law texts also contain many more passives than other texts. For example:

It is said that . . .

There is another reason why law texts appear so difficult: often they have grown over time. One law may be based on an older law that could be hundreds of years old. Much historical and social information would get lost if the law was rewritten in a simpler language. In addition, laws need to be very specific and explicit. It must be clear who the law applies to and what it covers.

Other examples

The language of textbooks is very different from the language you read in newspapers, novels and letters. Once you start your future profession, whether it is accounting, architecture, computer programming, business or law, you will find that some of the specialised subject language will also be used in the workplace. This means that as you learn new words you are storing them up for the future, not just for your time at university.

For example, if you are studying psychology you will be meeting words like these:

    attenuation theory
    sociopathy
    monomania

If your subject is physics you will be reading about:

    entripetal acceleration
    Larmor precession
    quantum chromodynamics

Don't worry! New words do not arrive like this in lists. You meet them in the chapters of your textbook where the rest of the sentence helps you to make sense of the meaning. You hear new words in lectures where someone is explaining the meaning with diagrams and other examples.

Let's look at some differences between general English and the language of your textbooks.

Everyday words with special meanings

Many everyday words are used in special ways in different areas of study. Here's one example. You probably know the word 'subject' in its grammatical meaning.

    The subject of the sentence is . . .

But in many studies the word 'subject' means a person. For example:

    In this study the subjects were male adults between the ages of 30 and 35.

Here, the 'male adults' are called the subjects, because the research was about them.

Here are two more examples of quite ordinary words with special meanings.

What do you think is the meaning of 'given'? The chances are that you are thinking of sentences like these:

    Have I given you this handout yet?

    We were given three examples yesterday.

In everyday English 'given' is part of 'to give'. In science texts, however, it is used as an adjective:

A given bottle contains 500 ml of . . .

The meaning here is not that a bottle was given to someone, but that 'One possible bottle [which we can't see at the moment] contains 500 ml of something.' This is different from a bottle we know about or can see. It's also different from any bottle you might have on your kitchen shelf. It means 'the bottle used for this experiment'.

That is just one example. Here is another. Think of the word 'root': What does it mean to you? In everyday use it means a vegetable, to dentists it means a part of a tooth, and in mathematics it means the number you have to multiply by itself to get to the new number, as in:

The square root of 9 = 3.

These are just two examples of words that can have a special meaning in your subject. Most subjects, such as psychology or biology, have developed special ways of writing. We call these *conventions*, meaning that all psychologists and biologists follow them. Because everyone knows what to do, the rules are often not written down. That, of course, makes them difficult to learn, even for native speakers of English. How can you learn these patterns or conventions? Most people learn them by reading many texts in their subject.

Written words, spoken words

Another difference you will notice as you read and listen to lectures is that some words are usually used in talking and others are more often found in writing. These words and phrases might have the same meaning, but speakers often say something one way while writers say it another way. Table 6 gives some examples.

Let's look at some of the differences in more detail. When we talk, we mention ourselves (I, we) but when we write in academic (university) language the 'I' and 'we' often disappear. Instead, writers use what we call the 'passive':

X can **be** explain**ed** by . . .

Y and Z need to **be** consider**ed**.

Another difference is that when we speak we use question words, such as 'how' and 'why', but in writing we tend to use nouns, such as 'explanation'

Table 6   Written words, spoken words

You hear someone say . . .	In the textbook you read . . .
I have no idea how we got these results.	An explanation of these results is unclear.
Now we've shown why it happens.	The causes have now been explained.
That's another story.	That is a separate topic.
We need to think about other possible reasons.	Other factors need to be considered.

and 'causes'. Also, speech has more 'ordinary' words like 'another' and 'story', whereas writing has less common words such as 'separate' and 'topic'.

Word pictures

Many words can be used in two ways, figuratively (like a picture) or literally (in their original meaning). Most languages also use words to paint pictures. When someone says 'Let's not dig up that subject,' you picture someone with a spade, digging in the garden to find something under the earth. Really the speaker is talking about finding out things that are out of sight. When we use words literally they are used in their first meaning. For example 'a field' is a place where farmers grow food. However, in university language 'field' has other meanings too, such as 'a field of study', 'a field of interest'. Thus your lecturer might say 'That's not really in my field. Try asking Dr . . .'. This use is called a *metaphor* or *figurative language*.

Metaphors are used in many subjects. Can you think of examples in your own language? Here's an example from English.

In a medical course the students were looking at the results of a test of two groups of people who had the same problem. The first group were given real medicine and the second group had something that looked the same, but which was not real medicine. When the students saw the results, they didn't know which people had been given which. Their lecturer said, 'We've blinded the results.' Then when everyone had looked at the results of the tests the lecturer said, 'Now we are going to unblind the test.'

You can probably figure out what 'to blind' means and then also what 'unblind' means. English uses many of these metaphors in writing and in speaking.

Abbreviations

Academic language is full of 'words' that are really letters standing for something else. Many people who use the initials understand what they mean but couldn't tell what the letters actually stand for. Here are some examples:

DNA = deoxyribonucleic acid   *Example*: The police used a DNA test to solve the crime.

ECG = electrocardiagram   *Example*: The doctors looked at the ECG to check the patient's heart condition.

RSI = repetitive strain injury   *Example*: The doctor said she had RSI because she worked on the computer too much.

Most people have no idea about the whole word or phrase, although they use the initials quite often.

As we will see in Chapter 9, other abbreviations are commonly used to make writing easier and quicker, particularly in emails, such as:

FYI = for your information
BTW = by the way

▶ Steps in learning new words

Some people say that just learning new words the way we do with our first language is good enough. Gradually as we read and listen we'll know more words. Many tests have been done to see if trying to learn words makes students remember them better, and it seems that trying does help more than just waiting till you know them from reading and listening. For the second part of this chapter we look at ways of helping yourself to increase the number of words you understand and know.

Choosing words to learn

If you are deciding to try and 'learn' some new words, then you need to make some decisions. The first one is, 'Which words are worth learning?'

In lectures and tutorials you hear people talking about your subject. Here are some of the places where you will find the written language of your subject:

your text books;
class handouts;

articles from the Internet;
articles from special journals.

Remembering new words
Here are some of the ways that students say they remember new words and their meanings.

1. Make lists with explanations in English or your own language.
2. Think of interesting ways to remember meaning, such as sounds, rhymes and pictures.
3. Learn the meaning of common word starters (prefixes) and word endings (suffixes) in English and group similar words together (see Chapter 6 for more on this topic).
4. Try to work out the meaning for yourself first.

This last point needs explanation. When you come to a new word, what do you do first? Many students turn quickly to their dictionaries but the dictionary is not always a great help, especially if you are using a small electronic dictionary which often only has one or two meanings for each word. Another difficulty is that words do not have meanings just by themselves. They get their meaning partly from the words around them.

Even if your dictionary is really good, there is a reason for not using it immediately. Research shows us that when readers try to work out the meaning of the word on the page by asking themselves 'What is that word most likely to mean?' before looking it up in the dictionary, they remember it better.

Learning words from electronic articles
We have already mentioned that some of your reading is available electronically. In that case, here is a way to learn new words from the article.

1. Find an article that your lecturer has recommended.
2. Bring it up on the screen.
3. If you can, copy this electronically to your own documents.
4. Now you can look for answers to questions like these:

   • What are the most important words? (Check how often these are mentioned.)
   • Which phrases do these words appear in most often? (Which words go before and after the important word?)

For example, we talk about

> *a major crisis, a major decline*

but

> *a grand event, a grand scheme*

When you start to use words yourself, rather than just understand them when others use them, you come across another problem. Your dictionary may tell you that several words have the same meaning: *big, major, grand.* . . . When you start comparing them, though, you find that they don't all go with the same words.

In English many words are always followed by particular prepositions, such as *to, by, from, with*. See if you can find four examples in this paragraph. You will learn these gradually as you read more. When you are writing essays a good dictionary will help you with these words but the essay marker should not have too much trouble understanding your meaning if you do make mistakes with some of these smaller words.

Starting to use the new words

As you start to learn a new word start using it in your writing (assignments and lab reports) and saying it (in tutorials or in laboratory work). This is one way of helping yourself remember the word and, of course, it's a way of writing a good assignment.

Some students are afraid to start talking. They think: 'Maybe people won't understand me.' Try not to worry about this too much. Many students make mistakes in saying new words even in their own language. If you say them, someone else can correct you. If you are not sure, ask someone, 'How do you pronounce that word? I've never heard it said.'

▶ Two students' stories

To end this section we hear from two students who went overseas to study, and we learn how they improved their language. The first student had already learned English as a second language when he decided he wanted to learn Arabic. He took himself to an Arabic-speaking country. After each part of his story there are questions to help you think about whether his story has any ideas you could copy.

> *I wanted to have a teacher as well as studying by myself. I preferred this over attending a special language course that might conflict with my courses at university. Also, I found that most of the language courses they told me about were either very expensive or didn't match my needs. I had*

studied Arabic before and knew pretty well what I needed to improve and therefore decided to get a private teacher for a few hours per week and study by myself for the rest.

1.   Do you know exactly what you need, to improve your English?
2.   Would you like to have a one-to-one teacher?

To find a teacher I visited the French Cultural Centre, the British Council and several embassies to look on their noticeboards and to ask the people who work there if they could recommend anyone. That's also when I found that the American cultural centre had a small self-access centre with some resources that you could use for a small fee. On the noticeboards I found some people who wanted to learn English. I decided to call some of them and with one I started a language exchange; I taught him English for the first hour and then he taught me Arabic for the second.

3.   How would you describe your needs briefly on a noticeboard?
4.   Would you be interested in teaching your language at the same time?

I had the names of some teachers so I tried them and agreed with them that we would try for one or two lessons first. Not all teachers had a teaching style that I felt comfortable with. Some were very good at Arabic but had little experience in teaching. Others had not attended university and were therefore not able to teach me the Arabic I would need to listen to lectures, write assignments etc. But eventually I found some good teachers. I chose one teacher to help me with the Syrian dialect, one for academic Arabic and one for reading and poetry. These were the areas they were good in and that they liked to teach. It also gave me a chance to get used to their different ways of speaking.

5.   How would you find out if a person was the right teacher for you?

Especially in the beginning I tried to use my newly acquired skills as much as possible in public. I went to markets instead of the supermarket as it gave me more opportunities to speak. I went to a local café quite often and got to know the people there. There was a storyteller there (not a very common profession!) and his stories must have been great, judging by the level of laughter in the audience. In the beginning I didn't understand much of what he said but I vividly remember the day when I first understood a joke. It was a great reward. I also went to a church, something I normally never do, just to get used to the local dialect. For the same reason I listened to the Friday prayer in the neighbourhood mosque. Oh, and I shouldn't forget the bath house. Going to the bath house is a social event in Syria where

*men (and women at separate times) come together to drink tea, take a
hot steam bath and just chat and have a relaxing time. Whenever I
went there alone I was sure to find someone to talk to. There was no
television in our home but I listened to the radio a lot and bought the local
newspaper.*

6. Where could you go to practise English?
7. Are there any activities you don't normally do but that you could try?

*In a few weeks I started feeling more confident. After I had been practising
Arabic for academic purposes with one of my teachers I decided to attend
some public lectures at the university. Because they were public, they were
quite general which made them easier to understand. I chose topics that I
already knew something about because I had previously studied them in
my home country. I still remember the feeling of victory when I could actually understand part of what was being said!*

8. What chances could you find to sit and listen to English spoken on topics
    you know something about?

*After a few more weeks it was time for the real work when the new semes-
ter started and lectures began. I had great difficulty finding out where to go
to enrol and where my classes were. All I could find was a hallway full of
posters with illegible instructions. I think I asked at least a dozen students
and staff. In class, seating arrangements were not what I was used to. There
were at least 70 students in a small classroom. The only air conditioning
was an open window. Women sat on one side of the room, men on the other.*

9. Apart from language, what differences do you expect to find in the new
    university?

Another student's story
This chapter ends with an interview with a Japanese student who said he
had very little English before he went overseas for the first time, to the United
States. See if you can find any good ideas from his answers.

Question
How did you prepare yourself before going?

Answer
*I studied English for only three months. Of course we had English in school
but it was minimal. When I decided to go overseas I studied English for
TOEFL, so what I did was focus on grammar, reading and vocabulary and*

forget about pronunciation. After they accepted me I started studying by using books on how to write academic texts and things like that.

Question

So you must have had a lot of work to do to get up to the standard. Was it difficult?

Answer

After I arrived I often went to the library to read articles. I read them many times to look at how they were written. From those examples I learned to write academic texts myself.

Question

That's fine for reading and writing but it sounds a bit of a lonely life. What about friends?

Answer

I stayed in the International House where most people spoke English. In the second year I moved into a house with Americans and that's when I really started talking.

Question

How did you understand the lectures if you didn't know any English?

Answer

It was difficult but I used the handout. I read it carefully, many times after the lecture and I also recorded the lecture and listened back to it many times.

Question

Didn't you take any courses or did you take private lessons when you arrived?

Answer

No. In the second year some friends helped me with my English but in the first year I didn't know where to go in the university for help. There was a Writing Centre where people can help you to check your writing, but I didn't know about it.

Question

Did you find that your earlier study in Japan was a help?

Answer

In Japan at university officially I had lessons in English but in practice this didn't help much. There was a little bit of reading in English but hardly any speaking. The first year was very tough in terms of speaking and writing, especially academic writing because I had no experience in academic writing, not even in Japanese.

Question

Apart from the language, were there any major differences between studying in Japan and the States?

Answer

In Japan you don't need to really study to get a C or a D, you just need to attend. In the States you have to participate, write a lot of things, answer questions etc. just to get a C. Also in class in the States you have to really do a lot, have discussions, do presentations etc. . . .

Question

How did things work out for you in the end?

Answer

Quite well actually. After a few years I started working at the Writing Centre. I learned a lot by helping others.

As you can see from this student's story and from all the suggestions from other students in this chapter, there are many choices for improving your English. People try different ways of learning until they find the right one for them. If you have a private tutor but think that it would be more fun to learn in a class then arrange to try some classes. If you have been in a class for some weeks and it is not helping you, look at one of the other choices. Remember what we said at the start of this chapter. Your goals are your own. You can make them and break them.

Part II
Your University Studies

Introduction

In this second section of the book we describe the regular things students do at university as part of their studies. We could have called Chapters 4 to 7 'Listening', 'Speaking', 'Reading' and 'Writing' but that would be too simple. Although people think of lectures as a time for listening, they are really much more than that. As you will see in Chapter 4, lectures are also a time for writing and for making connections with what you have been reading. Similarly in tutorials (Chapter 5) students need to be good listeners if they want to be good talkers.

The final chapter of this section is for postgraduate students. This talks about the stages students work through as they put together a thesis or dissertation. This includes information about working with the lecturer who is your supervisor.

4 Lectures

In the first two chapters of this book you read about the planning you needed to do before starting your university studies and in Chapter 3 you read about ways of improving your English. The rest of this book is for students who know what they are going to study. This chapter explains what you can expect in lectures. You probably know that lectures are very different from school classes but you may wonder what these differences mean. In this chapter we look at ways to make understanding lectures and taking notes easier and more successful.

This chapter answers the following questions:

- What is the purpose of lectures?
- How are lectures organised?
- How can students take good notes?
- Do students ask questions in lectures?

▶ The purpose of lectures

Most university courses include weekly lectures, often in large theatres with the lecturer standing at the front talking to rows of students as they take notes and occasionally, as we shall see, asking questions. Each lecture is on one topic only, which is decided beforehand and is usually listed on the course outline. When you enrol for your course the first thing you will want to know is your lecture timetable. This may be in the university calendar or departmental handbook.

Lectures are different from school classes and they are different from other parts of university life. In lectures people mainly just listen and take notes instead of talking in groups or doing tasks as happens in secondary school. Another difference from school classes is the numbers. Lectures vary in size but in some first-year courses there may be hundreds of students in the same room. If the course is very popular the same lecture may be repeated two or three times during the week.

Students' views
Let's hear what some students think is the purpose of a university lecture.

> *I think lecturers should tell us everything they want us to know on the topic. How else can we pass our tests?*

This first student probably has a different idea from the staff about the purpose of a lecture. Maybe he or she is thinking back to school days when it was possible for the teacher to say everything students needed for a test. At university, on the other hand, learning is much wider and the lecturer will expect people to read the set books and other reading.

Here is another student's idea.

> *Some students told me it doesn't matter if you don't go to a lecture because it's all in the book. That seems strange. Why bother to have lectures if they don't say anything new?*

That student is asking a good question. There must be some good reasons for going or nobody would turn up. Let's hear from the staff.

Lecturers' views
We asked some university staff what they think lectures are for. Here are some of their answers.

> *We try to make difficult topics easier in our lectures.*

> *The idea is to interest students in topics so they'll go and read more.*

> *Lectures are a chance for students to hear opinions from people who have done research in such and such an area.*

> *Students could find out all the content of lectures by reading lots of books and articles. Coming to the lecture is a way of getting an overview.*

Even today, when many departments put information on a website for students, lectures are a big part of university life. Staff use lectures to:

- introduce new topics;
- make students interested in a topic;
- help students to think about the topic;
- highlight the most important points;

- tell students which other sources are worth reading;
- make difficult points easier to understand;
- encourage students to want to find out more;
- give examples to help students remember the topic;
- link this week's topic with last week's.

▶ How are lectures organised?

We can't say that all lectures follow the same pattern, but generally we can say that lectures will have an introduction, then the main topic and finally a conclusion. As well as the lecturer's spoken words there may also be hand-outs, overhead transparencies, a Powerpoint presentation, and lecturers also write on the board from time to time.

The introduction

At the very beginning of the lecture, a lecturer usually tells students what today's lecture will be about. Table 7 shows some ways of doing this.

Understanding the lecture can be quite difficult for students who speak English as a second language, as this person says.

I could understand all the words but I don't really know what the topic was.

The topic is usually announced beforehand in the course outline. In that case, you could prepare yourself by reading the textbook chapter on the topic, or thinking of questions you hope the lecture will answer and discussing those with other students.

Table 7   The lecture introduction

Listen for these words . . .	In other words . . .
I'd like to talk about . . . *What we're doing today is . . .* *This morning we'll start looking at . . .*	This is the topic.
In other words . . . *What they're saying is . . .* *So the question is . . .*	This is what the topic means. (The lecturer is explaining things.)
That's not the same as . . . *That's not what we really mean by . . .*	This is what it doesn't mean. Here is something similar but different.

At the beginning of the lecture you may be given the topic on the board or the overhead projector, or the lecturer may say what the topic is. Sometimes the topic is put in the form of questions like these:

What do we know about . . . ?

Why have people often tried to find out . . . ?

We call these 'rhetorical' questions, which means that nobody expects anyone except the lecturer to answer them.

In summary, the lecture introduction answers questions such as:

- What are we talking about today?
- Why is this topic important?
- What are the main words for talking about the topic?
- How does this topic link with other parts of the course?
- What is *not* covered in this lecture?
- How will the lecture be organised?

The body of the lecture

Once the topic has been given, the lecturer starts to explain it. You may even hear one point explained in two or three different ways. Listen for words like these:

This means . . .

In other words . . .

Another way of expressing that is to say . . .

When the lecturer uses these words you are hearing the same point again. Another way of making the meaning clear is through examples. Some lecturers also tell you what the topic does *not* mean. When a topic is very detailed it is easy to get confused.

In summary, in Table 8 there are some words to listen for in the body of the lecture. Let's look at each of these points in more detail.

1   A sub-topic

A sub-topic is a small part of the main lecture topic. How do you recognise the start of a sub-topic? One way is to listen for the words. Students find themselves waiting for the next time that Lecturer X says 'OK' or Lecturer Y says 'Right' to know when a new point is coming, but everyone has their own favourite words for introducing a sub-topic. You will start to recognise these from different lecturers.

Table 8 The lecturer's words and their meaning

Listen for these words . . .		In other words . . .
And that leads to . . . *We now come to look at . . .* *Right. Well, if we move on . . .* *What I'd like to do now is . . .* *OK, now . . .*	1	Here's a new topic.
For instance . . . *For example . . .* *One way this works out is . . .* *Let me give you an illustration.* *This means . . .*	2	Here's an example or an explanation.
According to . . . *X would have us believe . . .* *Y says . . .*	3	This is what someone else thinks.
I think this is . . . *The most interesting point here is . . .* *Let me just say in parentheses . . .*	4	This is what I think.
By the way . . . *I might say here . . .*	5	This is interesting but not important.
So where was I? *Well anyway . . .* *To get back on the track . . .*	6	Now I'm getting back to the topic.
So . . . *What I'm saying is . . .*	7	Here's a summary.

As well as listening for the words that announce the next topic you can look and listen for other signs, such as these:

- The lecturer may walk to a different spot at the front of the room.
- The lecturer's voice may change (go higher or lower).
- The lecturer may look up at the class.
- There may be a short space between sentences.
- The lecturer may turn to another page of notes.

2 Examples or explanations
One way of making the topic easy to understand is with examples. The example may be from the past or the present and from this country or another country.

In some subjects like geography or archaeology, the examples may be photographs presented through the computer (Powerpoint) or as overhead projections.

3 Other people's opinions about the topic

Although some university topics are about facts, many are also about opinions. Lecturers will tell what Person A thinks and what Person B thinks, A and B being people who have studied the topic and done research on it. Their names are important to remember so that you can read more about their work later (you will need exactly the right spelling to find them on the computer). Talking about one piece of research by one person may take up five minutes of the lecture. Sometimes students want a short, easy answer to the question 'Does that mean that X is . . . ?' but the lecturer may answer, 'That depends on how you define X', or 'A believes . . . but according to B . . .'.

4 The lecturer's views

At other times lecturers themselves may say what they think about topics:

> 'According to research my colleagues and I are doing at the moment . . .'

5 Extra comments to make students interested

At the start of this chapter we saw that one purpose of a lecture is to interest students in the topic. Lecturers do this in different ways, such as by telling a joke. These jokes or extra comments are not new points and you don't have to write them down in detail. Sometimes, though, writing a word or two may help you understand the point better and remember it later.

How can you tell when a lecturer is adding something extra? Look and listen for these signs:

- The lecturer may look up from his/her notes.
- His/her voice may change tone.
- Other students may stop writing and just listen.

6 Getting back to the topic

After the joke or the story or the extra comment, the lecturer may say something like 'Where was I?' The other way of knowing that the lecture is continuing is to watch the body language and listen to the voice. Perhaps lecturers look back at their notes or change back to their more formal lecturing style.

The conclusion of the lecture

You know that a lecture is coming to an end partly because all lectures must finish at a certain time. However, you will also know that it is coming to an end if you hear one of these ways of ending it.

A summary of today's topic
Many lecturers end by telling you what you have just heard:

And so we have seen . . .

Today we've been talking about . . .

In summary . . .

In a word . . .

The main point of the lecture
There has probably been one main point to the whole lecture. Towards the end the lecturer may remind the class of this.

The important thing to remember is . . .

The main point is . . .

Next week's topic
The lecturer may also end by looking ahead to next week.

Today we've looked at . . . Next week we'll . . .

Looking ahead . . .

▶ Listening to lectures

What's special about listening to lectures?
Most of us do plenty of listening in our lives, so why do we find it difficult to listen to lectures? There are differences between listening to lectures and most other kinds of listening.

* *In conversations* we have a turn at speaking as well as at listening, but in lectures the person at the front does all the speaking. It is true, though, that some lectures sound a bit like conversations because the speaker includes you in the conversation: *'You probably remember . . .'.*

* *When we listen to the radio or TV* we don't have to take notes. We can sit back and listen; 24 hours later we remember things that are important to us but we have forgotten the rest. In lectures there's no sitting back. Students have to work hard to take down the important points.

However, the lecturer and the newsreader may be the same in one way. Some lecturers actually read their notes, sentence by sentence. This may mean you don't hear many comments that are not important. It means that the speaker has planned not just *what* to say but also *how* to say it.

- *In language classes* students sometimes listen to dictations. The teacher slows down so you can take down every word. A lecture is not like a dictation. You are listening to a voice that doesn't stop or slow down as you write.

- *When we listen to speeches* we are listening for the main message rather than for the details. Some speeches try to make us do something ('Vote for me!'), while others try to make us feel something ('This is an important day for our country'). By contrast, in a lecture the students are not generally being asked to do or feel anything (except interest!). Instead the speaker wants them to know something ('This is important for you to realise').

- *Listening to a story* is another kind of listening, when we listen to people telling us interesting things that have happened to them. They might start, 'Listen to what happened to me on the way in this morning . . .'. We listen to the story and then at the end we might say something to show we were interested, but we don't need to repeat the story to anyone.

Students' listening problems
Because lectures need a special type of listening, students report problems. Here are some examples.

1. Understanding a 'new' accent
One thing students say is difficult about listening to lectures is understanding a 'new' accent. Maybe your high school English teacher talked with one kind of accent and now your lecturers use a different one. In English-speaking universities the staff come from many different countries and from different parts of the same country. This means that even though they are all speaking English, it may take a week or two to get used to their accents.

Suggestions

1. Look at the lecture topic on the course outline beforehand and make sure you understand the title.
2. Read the textbook chapter on the topic.
3. Think about the questions you think the lecturer will be answering.

2. Understanding fast talkers

A second problem can be the speed of the lecturer's talking. Some students don't even know if what they are writing down is one word or two.

Suggestions

- Ask if you can record the lecture on tape. Some lecturers allow recordings.
- Try to note key points like names, statistics and dates.
- Use a capital letter instead of writing the key word every time it is mentioned. For example, if the lecture is about water pressure just write WP each time.
- Make up your own shorthand system for common words. Here are some that are often used.

&	= and
#	= number
A = B	= A equals B
A $\Rightarrow$ B	= A leads to B
@	= at

- Use plenty of space on the page as you take your notes. Make lists and sketches. You can add details later from your textbook.
- Write down what you *think* you hear. Then later try saying it aloud if it doesn't make sense. Maybe 'be low', is really 'below', for example.
- Go over your notes later with another student. This is actually a good idea even if you have understood most of the lecture.

3. Understanding jokes

Another problem is understanding jokes. As you know from your own language, jokes depend on understanding the words but also on knowing a lot of things that are not said. Furthermore, jokes are not funny unless the speaker and the listeners like making jokes about the same thing. A joke about an animal could be funny in one country but offensive in another.

Suggestions

There is not too much you can do about jokes. It's annoying to see other people laughing and not knowing why, but some of the students who are laughing may not understand the joke either. People sometimes laugh along with the others just to look good. One day as you learn more about the country where you are studying and as your English improves, you will understand the jokes too. It takes time.

4. Getting used to a different system

Everyone who changes countries has to get used to new things: the food, the way of driving, and of course the language. You might think that lectures will be similar all over the world, but that is not always the case. Listen to these students.

> *Our lecturers at home helped us to take notes. They used to write a list of points on the board. That way you knew which was point 1, point 2 and so on. Here they just keep going on and on so you don't know where the next point came.*

> *We used to listen to our teachers without writing because they would hand out notes or say 'That's all in Chapter 8.' Here, if you don't get it down you're lost.*

> *Why don't they speak slowly? Our teachers used to dictate the notes.*

> *The problem here is you can't expect the same thing from all the lecturers. They all have their own styles.*

Suggestions

- Remind yourself that finding lectures difficult and strange is quite common for all first-year university students.
- Talk with other people, including native speakers of English, and ask them how they help themselves to understand lectures.

5. Listening, looking and writing at the same time

In lectures you are doing three things at the same time: writing, listening and looking. 'How can I write fast enough to take down all the important bits?', students ask. While lecturers are talking they may also be writing on the board, pointing to overhead transparencies and showing slides. Maybe there are handouts as well to refer to.

Suggestions

- Look up from your notetaking from time to time because, as we saw earlier, there are clues from the way the lecturer moves around.
- Listen to what the lecturer says about the handouts. Are they the same as the lecture or something extra?

6. Finding links between the lecture and the textbook

If you are better at reading English than at listening, then you may notice that the lecturer's words are sometimes different from the words in your textbook. Of course the important words for the subject will be the same, but not all the words that join the ideas. The same thing probably happens in your language. People write differently from the way they speak.

Suggestions

• Read the textbook chapter before the lecture.
• If you can't do that, read it soon afterwards, looking at your notes to see how they match.

Test yourself

To end this section, see if you can do this task. The lecturer's words (in Column 1) do not match their meaning in Column 2. See if you can match each phrase with the right meaning. [Answers are at the end of this chapter.]

Column 1: Words	**Column 2: Meaning**
(a) We should be careful not to think of x as y.	1 extra details
	2 next point
(b) [Lecturer walks away from notes and talks.]	3 a comparison and a contrast
(c) This leads to the point that . . .	4 a very important point
(d) It's a bit like yesterday's case but not quite the same.	5 non-example
(e) Now, where was I?	6 an explanation
(f) . . . and this is really the key.	7 back to the topic
(g) Let me now talk about x then we'll go on to y.	8 an example
(h) One of the most common instances is . . .	
(i) In other words . . .	

▶ **Taking notes in lectures**

Students always hope that they can take notes that will be clear enough for later study. Good notetaking is an important skill for university. In this section we answer questions that students often ask about notetaking.

Why take notes?

Some students take no notes in the lecture. They say it's better to sit and listen to everything. That may sound like a good idea but how many people can remember an hour's talk if they have no notes? We asked some students why they took notes and this is what they said:

It helps me read the textbook.

My mind doesn't walk off if I am writing.

Writing helps me think.

I use my notes to study for the tests.

What can go wrong with notetaking?
Students say there are three main problems with notetaking.

1. They can't write down enough.
2. They can't read their own handwriting later because they have to write so fast.
3. Even if they can understand their notes they never find time to go over them until just before the examination.

Having pages and pages of notes is not always the answer. It might be better to have a few notes that make sense rather than pages and pages that you can't read.

How do students take good notes?
We asked some students to give advice on good notetaking. Here are their answers:

Don't try to write down everything. Just note the key points.

Try to understand what is being said when taking notes.

Read the textbook chapters before the lecture.

Say to yourself 'What do I know about this already?'

Don't be afraid to ask other students when you miss a point.

Here are some students talking about how they like to take notes. Read what they say and then decide which ideas sound useful to you and which you think would be a waste of time.

Student 1
I try to listen to an idea and then write it down in my own words.

Student 2

Translating everything into my language seemed like a good idea at first but that took too much time. Now I just use my dictionary later if I don't understand a word.

Student 3

I go really fast and try to take down every word. My friend does the same. Then we go and have coffee and compare notes and fill in the missing bits.

Student 4

If the lecturer puts anything up on the overhead that's my time for writing really fast.

Student 5

After the lecture I do little drawings in the margin. That's my way of remembering things.

Student 6

I use lots of numbers and arrows and boxes to keep track of everything. The only trouble is when the lecturer says 'third point' I'm sometimes up to point 7. I've never been able to work out why.

Student 7

I spend a lot of time in lectures worrying because of all the stuff I haven't written down.

Some students take notes twice. The first time is in class as they listen, and the second time comes when they reread their notes after class and rewrite them more clearly. The advantage of this is that after the lecture (preferably on the same day) you will remember most of what was said in the lecture. As you rewrite your notes you can put down the most important points in words that are clear to you.

One teacher's advice

First-year Commerce course students at one university were asked how they took notes and what they did with them afterwards. Then they gave their notes to a teacher, who looked at them carefully. Table 9 is a summary of the problems the teacher noticed, along with suggestions for better notetaking.

Table 10 lists what the teacher said was good about the notes and why.

Planning your own notetaking

You have read about what other students do. Now it is time to plan your own notetaking. Use these questions to help you start planning.

Table 9 Weaknesses in notetaking

Students' notes	Suggestion
Kept repeating words like this: Principle 1, Principle 2 . . .	Save time by putting a general heading and then numbering each one, e.g. *Principles* 1. 2. 3. etc.
Left no margin	Difficult to read No space for adding details later
Used very small pieces of paper	Small handwriting difficult to read later
Copied quotes without '. . .'	Difficult to reference later in essays

Table 10 Good points in notetaking

Good point	Why is it good?
clear script	easier reading later
a diagram	faster notetaking
two colours	distinguishes main headings and sub-points
abbreviations	faster notetaking
underlining	easier reading later
plenty of space	room to add details from textbook later
capitals for headings	headings stand out
dates and figures	facts to revise later
symbols	faster notetaking

1. How much do you plan to write down?

    ☐ I want to write down everything the lecturer says.
    ☐ I'll try to write down only the important things.
    ☐ I'll copy everything from all the overhead transparencies.

2. Why do you take notes in lectures?

    ☐ To save time so I needn't read so much.
    ☐ To help me think about the topic.
    ☐ To help me understand the textbook.

☐ To prepare me for further reading.
☐ To guide me in preparing for tests and exams.

3. How will you use your notes later?

☐ I'd like to rewrite them.
☐ I'll read them at least once.
☐ I won't use my notes. I'll ask to see other people's notes.

4. You can answer this question if you have already started notetaking in lectures.

☐ I wish I could take down more.
☐ I can understand the lecturer and take notes at the same time.
☐ I am usually too busy writing to think about meaning.
☐ I worry about missing points as I wrote.

▶ Asking questions in lectures

Lectures are mostly a time for listening. However, lecturers do sometimes invite questions and a few students respond.

Why ask questions in lectures?

When the class is very large, as in many first-year courses, you might wonder why any student would be brave enough to ask a question. Of course most students don't ask questions. They say 'I'm too shy,' or 'I'm not smart enough,' or 'The lecturer won't understand me,' or 'Everyone knows the answer to this except me.' These reasons stop them from finding answers to their questions.

If you can forget your fears you may find that the lecturer's answers to your questions helped everyone in the class, not just you. Sometimes nobody understands a point the lecturer has said and everyone is pleased that someone is brave enough to ask the question. Once a question is asked, all the other students look up and listen.

Here is another reason for asking questions. When nobody asks anything, lecturers think everybody has understood that part of the lecture. Questions show them which parts were unclear or how to explain things better. That means in the next class the lecturer may give more examples or use clearer words and explanations.

When can I ask a question?

The usual time to ask questions is when the lecturer asks for them. That may be at the beginning, during, or towards the end of the class. In large lectures not many students interrupt with a question while the lecturer is talking. Listen for the lecturer to invite questions in words like those in Table 11.

Sometimes you are not sure whether or not to ask a question. Maybe the lecturer has said something like this without waiting long enough for anyone to put up their hand:

Now if that's clear we'll move on to the next topic.

Now look at the speaker's 'body language'. If lecturers put down their notes and look round the class as they invite questions then that probably means they really are willing to give answers.

You often see a little crowd at the front waiting to ask questions at the end of the class instead of when the lecturer invited them. If there is time for questions in class, then that's the best time to ask. For one thing, all the students can hear the answers. Another reason is that there is very little time at the end of class. If the room is needed for the next class or the lecturer has to go to teach somewhere else, your questions will have to be answered quickly in the corridor. If at the end of the class you still have an unanswered question then it is better to contact the lecturer at another time. In Chapters 9 and 10 you can find out which staff to contact and how.

Table 11   Invitations to ask questions

The lecturer says . . .	Explanation
Last week we discussed . . . Does anyone want to ask anything about that . . . ? *Any questions?* *Anything you want to discuss?*	These questions come at the start of the lecture. If you have read your lecture notes and still don't understand them, now is the time to ask.
Is everything clear so far?	This question comes during the lecture. You can ask about something the lecturer has just said.
Would anyone like me to go over that once more?	Here the lecturer has explained something difficult. If you didn't understand, now is the time to ask.
Does that help?	This question follows the lecturer's answer to a question. Students usually say 'Yes thanks,' but if they haven't understood, this is the time to ask.

Let's say that the lecturer has invited questions and that you have something to ask. What happens next? How do you know if it's your turn to ask a question? Just watch for the first couple of weeks and you'll soon see what everyone else is doing. In small classes the student might look at the lecturer and then the lecturer names that person, but in bigger classes the most common way of getting a turn is:

1. put up your hand; then
2. wait for the lecturer to point to you;
3. call out your question clearly.

Usually lecturers answer the question immediately. Occasionally, though, they might say something like this: 'Good question. We're coming to that in a few minutes.' Or the lecturer might check first how many people want an explanation by asking, 'How many of you would like me to explain that?' If nobody else puts up a hand, the lecturer might ask the questioner to stay for a moment at the end.

What sort of questions do students ask during lectures?
Here are some examples of students' questions.

1. Questions about details
If you don't understand a word or phrase that is repeated through the lecture and seems to be important, then you can ask:

What does X mean?

Excuse me but what do you mean by Y . . . ?

Please could you explain once more . . . ?

Other questions remind the lecturer that something has not been quite clear. Notice the words *'Excuse me'* and *'Please'*. Students who don't use words like these in their own language think that English speakers overuse them, but they are a quick way of making yourself sound more polite and friendly.

2. Questions about the textbook
Lecturers like questions that show students have been thinking and reading between classes. Here are examples:

On page __ of the course book it says __ How is that related to today's lecture?

Could you explain the point about __. in our book?

3.   What sort of questions is it better not to ask?

Some students ask a question that has just been answered. This can happen if you have been waiting for some time to ask your question and have forgotten to listen to what the lecturer is saying while you wait for your turn. Students sometimes ask 'When is the next assignment due?' when the date is written on the board. A few questions about feelings or personal opinions are better asked in tutorials, such as:

How do you feel about . . . ?

What do you think about . . . ?

What if my English is weak?

Some students who speak English as a second language worry that nobody will understand their questions. Here are three ideas for asking clear questions.

1.   Speak loudly

In a large lecture room you need to speak up. When people feel shy about their English they sometimes whisper their questions and the lecturer has to ask them to repeat what they have said. If you want to be heard the first time round, speak loudly.

2.   Make the question short and simple

Clear questions are usually short. Plenty of native speakers of English ask questions that are unclear because they are too complicated. Look at the difference between these two questions:

I was wondering about what you just said and I was thinking that maybe that's why . . . but on the other hand maybe it's not.

Is that why . . . ?

In the first example the student is really thinking aloud rather than asking a question. This kind of thinking is helpful in a tutorial (see Chapter 5), where there is time for people to think and to hear one another's views.

3.   Keep to the topic

Try to make your question on today's topic rather than one that will be covered in one of the next lectures. Again, tutorials are the place for asking more general questions.

Don't worry about your English
When you ask a question, the lecturer is interested in *what* you are saying rather than *how* you are saying it.

Answers to the task on p. 75.

    a = 5 non-example;
    b = 1 extra details;
    c = 2 next point;
    d = 3 a comparison and a contrast;
    e = 7 back to the topic;
    f = 4 a very important point;
    g = 2 next point;
    h = 8 an example;
    i = 6 an explanation.

5 Small Group Learning

In the last chapter we explained why lectures are important. However, they are not the only way that students learn. You will also learn in small groups. In this chapter we discuss four types of small groups: tutorials, laboratory sessions, student-led seminars and joint projects. Talking is important in all of these groups.

This chapter answers the following questions:

- When are students expected to talk at university?
- What is the purpose of tutorials?
- What to say during laboratory work.
- How do students work together on seminars and joint projects?

▶ Tutorials

As well as lectures, many subjects have tutorials once every two or three weeks. They are smaller than lectures and students have more chance of getting to know one another.

What are tutorials for?
So far we have talked about large classes, but many courses have tutorials too. As well as being smaller than lectures, tutorials are often taught by different staff. Tutorials have several purposes, all of them to do with talking:

- to discuss the lectures;
- to exchange opinions about course readings;
- to work on group assignments;
- to discuss assignments;
- to ask questions.

Look in your departmental handbook or listen to the tutor on the first day of class to see what your subject teachers believe is important about tutorials.

The purpose of a tutorial is to talk, because talking is one way of learning. Another reason for everyone talking is to make the learning more enjoyable. If only two or three students speak, the tutorial can become boring.

Here are reasons why some international students said they liked to talk in tutorials.

Talking puts me in the group. If I don't talk nobody talks to me afterwards. Everyone says 'Coming for coffee?' to the talkers but they leave the quiet people alone.

I stop worrying if I talk about my problems.

Actually I talk to make my English better. I don't care if my English isn't great. It's like riding a bicycle. If I don't try I won't get better.

I think the tutor notices the people who talk. It's good. She starts to say our names.

To understand something. That's why I talk. I don't understand a new thing properly if I don't talk about it. The other day a student said afterwards, 'Is that what it means? I didn't understand it till you talked.' That shocked me because I thought I didn't understand it myself.

There is another reason for speaking. When you leave university and work in your profession, you will probably have to do some speaking to large groups. Small tutorials are a good chance to practise speaking in front of other people.

Making people talk in tutorials is only partly the tutor's job. If students decide they don't want to talk then it's very difficult to make them.

Why do some students keep quiet in tutorials?
Many students sit in a tutorial week after week without saying anything. Why is that? Maybe they do not know the purpose of a tutorial. They think it is like a small lecture where the teacher gives them information. Even if students do know what a tutorial is for, there can be other reasons why they keep quiet. We'll talk about their reasons under four headings, dealing with students' language problems, the tutor, differences in the ways students communicate, and finally, students' lack of confidence. As you read them you could ask yourself whether any of these apply to you.

1.   Language worries

People who speak English as a second language often think other people won't understand them. They say:

> *My English isn't very good. When I speak it's hard for people to follow. It's better if I keep quiet.*

It's easy to think that nobody understands you but there are two answers to that. If you don't speak then you will never improve. It's better to have someone say 'I beg your pardon,' so that you can try again, than to keep quiet for ever. The second answer is this. Even in their own language everyone has times when people don't understand them. It's a part of communication. Just try saying the same thing in a slightly different way.

Another reason for not speaking is shyness. You probably think that all the students who speak English as their first language feel confident all the time but they don't. They can also worry about shyness. If everybody thought about problems of understanding and shyness in tutorials there would be no interesting talk and less understanding of the whole topic.

When you speak, people are interested in *what* you say more than *how* you say it. Speak clearly and say something short the first time if you want to build up your confidence.

2.   The tutor doesn't include everyone

Unfortunately some tutors do not make it easy for everyone to join in. Sometimes they are so pleased to have anyone speaking that they forget to include all students. As a member of the group you can do something about this. Don't wait to be asked; just speak. Remember that tutors who are actually senior students themselves may feel just as nervous as the students at the start of the year.

3.   Intercultural communication

Another reason why some students say very little in tutorials relates to different 'rules' for talking in different cultures. As two students said:

> *I don't know when it's my turn to speak.*

> *Every time I leave a space before speaking, someone else comes in and fills that space.*

This really can be a problem. It's not always clear who is supposed to be speaking and how to get a turn. Here are the three most common ways people get a turn.

- Look at the tutor so he or she knows you are ready to speak.
- Start speaking as soon as the last person stops speaking.
- Say 'Can I say something?'

4.   Feeling stupid

There is one more reason why some students keep quiet. Many students new to university think:

> *I've got nothing important to say. If I try to speak people will laugh at my ideas.*

> *Everyone here is smarter than me. What if I say something stupid or wrong?*

In every group there are students who think like this. The advice of a student who used to feel stupid but now takes turns at speaking is this:

> *At first I started speaking really quietly and just said a few words. Then I found out that I wasn't more stupid than everyone else. I wasn't cleverer either. Just somewhere in the middle.*

Ways of joining in tutorials

If you have decided that you want to be one of the talkers, then read this discussion amongst students who have just seen a film (movie). The teacher has asked them to get into a group and talk about cloning (cloning means 'to make an exact copy of a plant or animal by taking a cell from it and developing it artificially').

Student 1:   Okay, do you agree to cloning human beings? Why or why not?

Student 2:   I think I could not agree to it because if you just copy yourself you could not copy your mind. Just, just how do you face the copied guy?

Student 1:   Hmm, terrible, I think.

Student 3:   And I don't agree with this about clone human beings because we are developing these areas. If we can take a good gene, or the best genes from human beings we may make only good people. So there is no distinction between good and bad people.

Student 4:   I agree with this.

Student 1:   Okay. Any more? Any more ideas?

Notice that one student seems to be the leader. When you have a small group, it sometimes helps if one person has the job of helping others to speak. Even if you are not the leader there are things you can do to keep the talk going. Let's look at some of them.

1.   Agree with the last speaker
The most common (and the easiest) way of keeping the talk going is to agree with what someone else is saying. Say something like 'That's right. Yes, Okay,' or even 'Uhuh.' Even if you do not feel ready to speak up yourself you can agree by saying something like this:

I was thinking that myself.

Yes, I know what you mean.

2.   Add information
Of course if everyone simply said 'That's right,' the tutorial would soon stop. You can add to the last speaker's remark to keep the topic going. Try saying one of these:

Yes, that reminds me . . .

I have another example of that . . .

There's something about that in Chapter . . .

3.   Ask for more information
If you are interested in what another student has just said, ask for more information:

Do you have any other examples of that point?

What do you mean by . . . ?

Are you saying that . . . ?

What does that mean exactly?

Sorry, I don't quite get your meaning.

4.   Give opinions
What do you think about the topic being discussed? Putting your opinions into words is another way of keeping a discussion going. Opinions are usually introduced with phrases like these:

I think . . .

It seems to me . . .

In my opinion . . .

Your opinions don't have to be permanent; in fact many people use language that shows they are not absolutely sure:

I was wondering if . . .

Do you think that perhaps . . .

Just supposing that . . .

It could be that . . .

Maybe it's . . .

5.   Disagree with something

Part of tutorial discussions is disagreeing with a point someone has just made. This is not quarrelling, as some students think. As we saw in the examples about giving opinions, the person disagreeing may not even be sure that he or she does disagree. Putting doubts into words is one way of finding out what you think yourself and thinking of new ideas as a group. For example, you can say:

That doesn't seem right to me.

Maybe . . . but I think it's more likely that . . .

Sorry. I don't agree. I think . . .

6.   Show interest in what the last person has said

Even if you have nothing new to say yourself, you can keep the conversation going by showing interest like this:

Really?

Is that true?

7.   Learn from others

When you are at a tutorial, start listening to all the ways students join in. Here are some points to watch for:

* How do people get a turn to talk?
* How do they show that they are listening to one another?

- How long does each person usually speak for?
- What words do they use to question other people's ideas?
- What words show they are not sure if their own ideas are right?

▶ Laboratory work

Working with other students in laboratories, usually in groups of twos or threes, is often an integral part of courses in psychology and many other science subjects. As well as your fellow students, there will be one or more teaching assistants to help you. These assistants are usually postgraduate students who try and answer questions or make suggestions. Remember, though, that they don't know as much about the topic as senior staff and they may not be able to answer all your questions.

Most of the talk during laboratory time is about the work, but sometimes there is social talk too. Of course not everybody likes talking about other things during the laboratory work. Some find it difficult to talk about other things at the same time. Here are some ways of talking about your work.

Make suggestions
Laboratory work depends on cooperation. That means each person should make suggestions about what to do next.

What would happen if we . . . ?

Let's try . . .

How about if we . . . ?

Shall we . . . ?

Ask someone to do something
You can also ask the other person to do something. Some of these examples sound like questions and some sound like orders but they are the normal way of talking about work.

Can you hold this?

Would you mind . . . ?

If you write that down, I'll call out the numbers.

Why don't you . . . ?

Describe what is happening

At the end of the laboratory work you will probably write a report. This report will be easier to write if you think aloud with your work partner as you go along.

It looks as if . . . [something is happening].

That must be the same as . . .

What's the difference between . . . and . . . ?

Where do you think . . . ?

Why is that happening?

Look at . . .

Ask questions

From time to time you can check that you are all doing the right thing, like this:

Are we supposed to . . . ?

Is that thing working properly?

What are we meant to do next?

Where do we go from here?

What's next?

Ask others to agree

One way to invite someone to agree with you is by using what we call 'question tags' ('isn't it?' 'do we?' 'haven't you?' etc.)

We haven't got that right yet, have we?

That doesn't look right, does it?

Agree and disagree

As we saw in the tutorial talk, don't be afraid to agree and disagree with one another.

That's not right. Look . . .

No, no. Just compare these two.

I don't think that can be right.

That doesn't look right to me.

▶ Seminars

A seminar presentation means that one student or a group of students stands at the front of the class and gives information to the other students. Seminar presentations can make many students very nervous, whether or not their first language is English. On the other hand you may be someone who enjoys the challenge of talking to a group of students and making your talk as interesting as possible.

Some time before, you will be given seminar guidelines which tell you:

- the topic or choice of topics;
- the length of the seminar;
- ideas for support material (overheads, handout pages, etc.).

Here are some very general tips for enjoying and making the most of your seminar, based on students' experiences.

Preparing for the seminar
Although it is impossible to prepare everything beforehand, here are some general ideas about preparing for a seminar.

1.   Don't try to memorise your talk
For most students it's a waste of time to learn a talk by heart. They would be better taking the time to organise interesting ways of presenting their ideas, such as planning examples or overheads. Students generally prefer listening to someone talking sincerely rather than making a speech. Furthermore, the teacher does not give any marks for memorising.

However, some students are very good at memorising and they may prefer to learn their presentation by heart. If you are one of these, make sure you look around the audience as you talk.

2.   Have some 'props'
'Props' are things that take people's attention away from you. In a seminar presentation these could be any of the following:

- pictures on the overhead projector;
- short audio recordings;
- handouts;
- a computer presentation (a Powerpoint presentation).

Sometimes people use a computer when they do a presentation. They show computer programs, movies and slide shows. Many people use a program called Microsoft® Powerpoint or other programs that let them show pictures and text as well as sound and animation. This can be a great way of focusing your listeners' attention. Just occasionally, though, people use so many exciting and colourful ways of presenting the message that the audience remembers all the tricks but not the message itself. The other thing that can go wrong is that people don't practise their presentation and everyone has to wait while they sort out a technical problem.

3. Look at the audience
People enjoy listening more if they can see you looking at them rather than looking down at the paper or, worse still, hiding behind the page. Also, looking up from time to time helps to slow you down.

4. Think about timing
You will need to practise speaking at a speed that is easy to listen to. If you have memorised something it is easy to speak too fast as you hurry to get finished. Of course the timing is never the same twice because other students may ask questions or you may take longer showing the overheads. It's a good idea to plan which part you will/can miss out if time runs out. It is better to drop one more point in the middle than to finish suddenly without your summary or the Question Time.

5. Keep it all together
It's a good idea to write the structure of your presentation down so that you won't forget anything and so as to keep to a logical order. Table 12 shows one suggested structure.

6. Structuring a presentation
Below is some more information on how to structure your presentation. This is the advice given to students in one self-access centre.

Structuring a Presentation

The effective organisation of a presentation is essential if the audience is to follow without difficulty. A presentation needs to be divided into sections and a good presenter uses expressions to show their audience how they are dividing it. These expressions can be found in your Language Bank. The Presentation Plan shows you how to divide the structure of your presentation.

The introduction of a presentation needs to be dynamic to attract the audience, and needs to be clear to focus the audience. It is important to start your presentation with a greeting. This opens a friendly channel of communication. This should be followed by the title or topic and the purpose of the presentation. This allows the audience to focus on what you want them to gain from listening to you. You then need to inform the audience of the overall content by stating the main points precisely and concisely. This tells the audience the structure of your presentation and the way in which information is broken up into sections. Remember to state when the audience may ask questions, either to interrupt you as you speak or at the end of the presentation.

In the main body it is important to show when you are introducing the first point and subsequent points. For the audience it is much easier to follow your presentation. This is because it highlights the structure of the presentation and the information is broken up into sections, making comprehension easier. For the presenter, it not only highlights the structure, but also reminds him or her of where s/he has reached.

The ending needs to be dynamic too so that the presentation leaves a lasting impression on the audience and the key points are remembered. The ending is normally made up of three elements. First you should signal you are coming to the end by way of summarising what you have said. This pulls all the pieces together for the audience. This should be followed by concluding remarks and/or recommendations. This is what the audience takes away as significant and something to consider further. Finally, request any questions or comments for a smooth transition from the end of your presentation to the question phase.

Table 12 One presentation structure

Part of the presentation	Your notes
Introducing the topic: *Today I'd like to focus on . . .*	*Introduction*
Sequencing the points: *I'll be talking about X and then I'll . . .*	1. 2. 3.
Introducing first point: *My first point is . . .*	*Main part* 1(a) (b) (c)
Introducing a new point: *We also need to remember that . . .*	2(a) (b) (c) 3(a) (b) (c)
Finishing: *To sum up, I've given you eight points to show that . . .*	*Summary* Your final statement

7. Practising the seminar presentation

When you have finished writing an outline and know what you want to say, you could practise your presentation in front of a mirror or with some of your friends. If you have a tape recorder or a video recorder you could record your presentation so you can look at it later. Make this practice as 'official' as possible. Ask your friend(s) to sit down facing you. Ask them not to interrupt you but to tell you their comments afterwards. If you practise with a friend it is important to get good feedback. Ask your friend to answer the following questions:

Could you understand what I said?

Did I speak at the right speed?

How can I improve my presentation?

If you want to be more formal, the list of comments below will help you and your friend to find out what points you need to improve.

Pronunciation

D grade   *Did not speak clearly and I could not understand very much.*
C grade   *Did not speak clearly and I could understand only parts.*
B grade   *Spoke quite clearly but sometimes I could not understand words.*
A grade   *Pronunciation clear and correct. I understood everything.*

Grammar

D grade   *Sentences were mostly grammatically incorrect.*
C grade   *Many grammatical mistakes.*
B grade   *Some grammatical mistakes, but on the whole quite good.*
A grade   *Sentences grammatically correct.*

Vocabulary

D grade   *Used words in the wrong way.*
C grade   *Did not use many different words and often did not use them in the right way.*
B grade   *Used quite a variety of words, but not always in the right way.*
A grade   *Used many different words correctly.*

Fluency

D grade   *Did not speak at a reasonable speed or make complete sentences. It was difficult to follow the talk.*
C grade   *Had difficulty in speaking for more than a minute and spoke quite slowly. Occasionally it was difficult to understand.*
B grade   *Sometimes hesitated or spoke slowly. In general it was quite easy to understand.*
A grade   *Spoke fluently and in long sentences without stopping.*

Structure of the talk

D grade   *The structure of the presentation was not clear. I did not know what the main points were or how they related to one another.*
C grade   *The structure of the presentation was not very clear. Sometimes I had difficulty understanding what the main points were and how they related to each other. I had to listen very carefully.*
B grade   *Now and then I found it difficult to understand what the main points were and how they related to each other but in general I think I understood it reasonably well.*
A grade   *The presentation was clear and I was able to understand what the main points were and how they related to each other.*

Content

D grade   *The content was not interesting.*
C grade   *Some parts were interesting but a lot of it was a bit boring.*

B grade   *It was mostly interesting.*

A grade   *It was very interesting.*

Way of presenting

D grade   *Not active or enthusiastic. Spoke in a monotonous voice. Did not use hands or face to make the presentation more lively.*

C grade   *The way of presenting was not very active or lively. Sometimes I felt bored by the monotonous voice.*

B grade   *The way of presenting was sometimes active but sometimes the voice was monotonous.*

A grade   *The way of presenting was active and lively. Spoke enthusiastically. Used hands and eyes to make the presentation lively.*

Presenting the seminar

1.   Useful phrases

You can use the phrases below when doing your presentation. If it helps you to be more confident you could learn these by heart.

To introduce the topic say:

> *Today I want to talk about . . .*
>
> *This morning I'm going to talk about . . .*

To indicate the order of your points say:

> *First of all . . .*
>
> *Next I'd like to discuss . . .*
>
> *Another point is . . .*
>
> *Moving on then to . . .*
>
> *Turning to . . .*
>
> *Finally . . .*

To present an opposite view, say:

> *Of course some people say . . .*
>
> *X has a different view. He/She believes . . .*

To summarise your points say:

> *To sum up then . . .*
>
> *In summary . . .*

To end your talk say:

> *That's all for now. Any questions?*
>
> *I'll finish there. I'm happy to answer any questions.*

If you don't know the answer to a question say:

> *That sounds interesting but I haven't really thought about it.*
>
> *That's a difficult one. Maybe* [name your lecturer] *can answer.*

If you don't understand the question say:

> *I'm sorry I don't quite follow.*
>
> *Do you mean . . . ?*

Here are some hints for making sure you enjoy yourself.

2.   Don't worry!

This is the hardest piece of advice to follow of course. Many students are so busy worrying about whether their English is good enough that they forget to enjoy the presentation. A pleasant smile will overcome plenty of small pronunciation slips.

3.   Encourage questions

A seminar often includes questions. If you have put a plan of the seminar on the board then you can show exactly where the questions come. Don't be afraid of saying 'Sorry, there will be time for questions later.'

▶ Joint projects

Many courses have group assignments. This will mean a lot of talking with other students, some of them native speakers of English and others second-language speakers from many different countries. Here are some tips on making the most of joint projects.

Brainstorm

The lecturer will probably give you written instructions about the topic and about how the group should work together. The first step is to collect every-body's ideas, however good or bad they sound at first. We call this process 'brainstorming'. Here is one way of doing it.

1. Each person writes down one topic sentence related to the subject. For example:

    SUBJECT
    TOPIC SENTENCE

2. Then the group takes turns reading out their sentences.

3. Other people say what they think about each person's idea as they are read out. As they listen they ask themselves questions. For example:

    Is this on the topic?

    Are the words clear?

    What should come next?

Agree on the roles of each person

At some time you need to plan roles. A role is the part you play in doing the assignment. Here are some questions to start the planning.

Who wants to search on the library database?

Who will be in charge of this part of the topic?

Is anyone good at proofreading?

Who has good ideas for presenting our work to the class?

Take your time

First of all, when you are speaking, don't let others make you feel embar-rassed about your English. Taking time to make yourself clear is part of working in a group. Everyone takes an equal part, the slow speakers and the fast speakers.

Ask other people to repeat what they have said

In small groups people often talk quite fast, leaving little time for others. If you don't understand what the other person is saying, don't always blame yourself. After all, even in your own language there are times when you don't understand. Don't be afraid to ask people to slow down a bit, or repeat what they have said, like this:

Could you speak more slowly please?

Sorry, I didn't hear what you said.

What was that? I didn't catch what you said.

Could you say that again please?

In this chapter we have looked at when students speak and what they say during tutorials and laboratory work. You have also read examples of how to talk with other students during seminars and joint projects. The most important advice is perhaps not to be too afraid to make mistakes. After all, practice makes perfect!

6 Reading

As we have seen so far, university study includes listening and speaking. This chapter is about another skill, reading, which often takes hours of students' time. For second-language speakers of English, reading is useful both for all the new ideas you learn and for the development of your English. As you read you learn new words and also how ideas are put together in academic writing. This, of course, improves your own writing as we'll see in Chapter 8. Some university subjects have more reading than others but reading is an important part of all university courses.

This chapter answers the following questions:

* How many different reasons are there for reading at university?
* What types of reading are available for university students?
* How do students find the right materials in the library?
* What are some different ways of reading?

▶ Reasons for reading

You will be reading to prepare for most of your assignments. Therefore the short answer to the question 'Why do people read at university?' is 'To learn something new.' Let's look now in more detail at why you will be doing plenty of reading as a university student.

Reading to understand the lecture

As we saw in Chapter 4, lecturers try to talk about new subjects in interesting ways that make a topic clear. However, for some students, including many second-language speakers who are not used to hearing spoken English, reading is an easier way to understand a new topic. See which of the two plans below works best for you.

Student 1 likes to read about a topic before the lecture. She finds it is easier to take notes when she understands something about a subject beforehand.

Student 2 likes to read the textbook after the lecture. He says that listening to the lecture gives him questions and then he goes to a book to find answers to those questions.

Reading to find answers to questions

As Student 2 says, it's a good idea to have questions in mind before you start reading. The questions may be for your assignments, or, as in the case of Student 2, they may be questions that came to your mind in a lecture. Perhaps, as we saw in Chapter 5, you need to know more because you want to join in tutorials. Here are two different students saying how they found answers to their questions through reading.

Student 3

Everyone in the history class was talking about the __ period but I didn't know when that was. I looked up the index of the textbook and there it was.

Student 4

The lecturer was always referring to this theory or that theory without explaining it. At first I couldn't track theories down in the textbook but I did find it in the index of one of the books on our reading list.

Your questions could be about facts or they could be about viewpoints (opinions).

1. Answers from research

One place to find answers to your questions is to read other people's research. Research is new work done by one or more people, usually published in a journal. As you read these journal articles you will find the details of recent studies that have been mentioned in a lecture or listed on your reading list. You will be able to quote this information in your essays.

2. Different people's answers

Opinions (also called views or viewpoints) are what people think, not what has been proved. For many questions in your university study people are not agreed on the answer. Perhaps your lecturer has said something like this: 'Some people believe . . . but you will also find that . . .'.

Knowing these different opinions helps you join in tutorial talk and write essays. Saying what you think is an important part of joining in tutorials, as we saw in Chapter 5, and reading about the opinions of other people is one way of preparing yourself for these discussions. Also, in your essays you need to give more than one person's ideas. To find these you need to *either* read several articles on the same topic, *or* read one article or chapter with a range of opinions.

Reading to improve your English

Finally, reading improves your English language. As well as learning about your subject, as you read books and articles you learn about the language you need for writing, particularly essay writing. You will learn words that are used in academic writing. These are not totally different from the words you hear spoken in lectures and tutorials or from the words you read in letters or newspaper articles or stories. You will also learn about organising ideas for particular types of writing.

Next time you pick up one of the books or articles on your reading list, try asking yourself 'Why am I reading this?' Perhaps your reasons will match some of the reasons we have discussed here.

▶ What do university students read?

If reading is so important, you may wonder where to start. In this section we describe different reading materials and how they can be helpful for your studies. In the next section we list and explain places where university students find these reading materials.

At university you will see the word 'literature' used very often. One meaning of this word is novels, short stories, plays and poetry written in a particular language, but the expression 'the literature' is also used in a different way to refer to what people have written in a particular subject. Thus a lecturer might say:

We can see from the literature that . . .

You'll need to read the literature to see . . .

According to the literature . . .

Here 'literature' means books and articles that have been published in that subject and which are important in understanding details of the course topics.

A book of course readings

Sometimes, at the beginning of a course, the lecturer gives classes a collection of photocopied readings, bound together like a book and called 'course readers' or 'books of readings'. These are usually articles or chapters from books and come as part of your course fees. They can be quite helpful because you don't need to spend a lot of time finding all the journals and books in the library and photocopying them. However, in most courses students are expected to do some more reading as well.

Books
Books are, of course, a major source of reading at university.

1. Prescribed or recommended books
At the start of the course, and in later lectures, you will be given lists with the titles of books that are important to your course. Some courses use one or two books as their main source of information. These may be called:

texts (or textbooks),
prescribed or *set* or *recommended* reading.

This means that all students have to have a copy of them.

2. Edited and single-author books
Books may be written by one or more writers. If each chapter in the book has a different author then we call it an edited book. On the cover you will see *ed.* or *eds* after the person's name. This is short for *editor* and *editors*. Editors find the articles, make sure they are in a similar format and usually write one or more articles or chapters, often the first and the last chapters.

Other books are written by one person. These may report the author's own work or summarise the work of many people, or both.

Journal articles
In your subject certain journals are important. These are published every year or even several times a year. Journals print articles on subjects which people are researching at the moment, and also 'state of the art' articles that sum up the work of many people. Table 13 shows the parts of a research article and why you might want to read it.

How do you decide if an article is worth reading? This is difficult to know when you start your studies but as you move through your degree you will start to recognise some 'famous' names. If you look at the end of the journal you will often find out something about the author.

Research reports
A research report is different from an article. It is usually longer and contains a detailed methodology (a description of how the researchers found

Table 13 Parts of a research article

This part of the article ...	Answers these questions ...
The abstract	What is this study about? What questions did the researchers ask? What did they find out?
The introduction	Why is this topic important? Who else has studied this topic? What are these researchers asking?
The literature review	What have other researchers written on this topic?
The methods	How was this study planned?
The results	What did the researchers find out?
The discussion, recommendations and conclusion	What do the results mean? Who is interested in the results?

the answers to their questions). Whereas articles are usually published in journals, research reports may be published as articles in journals only later. At other times the research was done by a company or the government and the results have been made public.

Theses
Finally, in the library you will be able to read theses which have been written at your university (see Chapter 9). Remember, though, that just because a thesis is in the library this does not necessarily mean that it is of a high standard.

Buying books
The university bookshop is the place to go if you want to buy books for yourself. For textbooks that you need to read all through the course, buying your own copy is a good idea if you can afford it. If the books are very expensive, students often share one between two or three people. This can work well if you are working in small groups to prepare your essays. If each person in the group buys one book, everyone can use three or four books for the price of one.

▶ Library catalogues

This section is for people who want to use the library for most of their reading. Especially at more advanced levels, students are expected to find their own reading materials. The lecturer will help by giving a list of titles and other details but the students then go to the library or onto the Internet and find what they need.

Your university will have one main library and perhaps smaller libraries for some departments. If you are studying Arts subjects, perhaps the general library has all the sources that you need, but if you are a student of Engineering you may find most of your extra materials in the engineering library rather than in the main library. First you need to know how to use the catalogues and databases. Then you can find your way to the journals and books.

Borrowing books

You will be able to borrow most of the books in the library if you are a student and have paid your fees at the university. However, reference books can definitely not be borrowed. You read them in the library and you can take notes or photocopy them for your own use only.

In some libraries there is a section where popular books are kept behind a desk for 'short loans' because many students are waiting to use them. 'Short' can be just one or two hours, so that all students have a chance to read the book. The short-loan books are usually listed in your course handouts. Because arrangements vary from place to place, you need to find out the system at your library.

Borrowing journals

Usually new journals are in a special section of the library. You can read them or photocopy an article but not take them away. Older copies are elsewhere on the shelves, probably bound together as if they were books and sometimes able to be borrowed. Later in this chapter you can learn more about finding articles in the library catalogue, on the computers.

Online catalogues

University libraries have computers with an online catalogue. This catalogue is a list of all the materials in the library, including books and articles. Sometimes you can search the catalogue from home, through the Internet. In fact many libraries now have their collections online and people can search them from anywhere in the world, even if they don't study or work at that university.

Databases

A database is a collection of information. More and more universities now give their students access to online library databases, which have references with information about books and articles, journals, newspapers etc. There is not a clear difference between a catalogue and a database. All catalogues are databases, but not all databases are catalogues. Catalogues list all resources in a library. Databases list all resources that exist, but they are not necessarily all in that library. So when a library gives students access to a database, this will help them find out if a book exists, but they may not be able to get it from their own library. For that they will have to search the library's catalogue.

Because more and more of these materials are now available electronically, you may be able to read them on the Internet or download them onto your computer and print them out. Often this facility is called 'e-journals' (electronic journals), although sometimes entire books are available. The library pays to let its members access the databases and e-journals. If you are not a student you cannot usually use this facility unless you sign up for the database or the e-journal yourself. Some companies give you access to a large number of databases and e-journals for a fee. Some work with a CD rom, others through the Internet.

Here are some sites that give you access to electronic materials:

www.e-journals.org

This lets you search for electronic journals.

gort.ucsd.edu/newjour

This site is called Newjour and lists many online journals.

Catalogues and online databases allow you to search for materials in a number of ways, such as:

TITLE   The name of the book or journal. Sometimes you can search for journals separately.

Type in the title without articles (a, an, the). If you know only some words of the title, it's better to use KEYWORD (see below).

SERIAL TITLE   The name of the journal.

The serial title may also be called the 'journal title' or 'periodical title' or 'series title'. This searches for titles of paper or electronic journals.

AUTHOR   The person(s) who wrote the book.

CALL NUMBER   The number or code that the library gives the book.

KEYWORD   An important word in the subject/title

If you know only some words of the title or if you want to know if there *are* any resources with those words in the title, then use this 'keyword' option.

Sometimes you read that you can *truncate* your search terms. This means that if you are not sure how to spell a word or want all possibilities, then you use * (or sometimes !). For example, by typing in 'learn*' you will find 'learning', 'learner', etc. Often here you can use BOOLEAN OPERATORS. These are words that allow you to make your search more specific, such as AND, OR, NOT. For example, 'business AND contracts' will bring up book titles like 'business contracts in the United States' but also 'commercial law and contracts: a business perspective'.

SUBJECT HEADING   The name of your topic.

Subject headings is a way of searching for resources by topic. The names of the topics are the same internationally.

To know which words to use you can ask a librarian for help or look them up in this list:

www.loc.gov/catdir/cpso/lcco/lcco.html

You have to be very precise. The subject heading 'animal beha*viour*' will not give you any results, but if you spell it the American way, 'animal beha*vior*', it will. Often there is an advanced search option that lets you combine some of these techniques.

If you want to look at libraries' catalogues then the following links will be useful:

sunsite.berkeley.edu/Libweb/

This site lets you search for libraries. Usually these libraries have online catalogues that you can search.

www.libdex.com

This site is similar to the previous one.

The Internet

The Internet is a great place to find reading materials as well as all sorts of other information that can help you in your university studies. For instance, you can find:

- research articles that you can read online;
- books that you can order online or request through a library;
- people interested in the same topics as you are.

Where to search?

How do you know where to search and how? The best thing to do is to use a *search engine*. This is a special webpage that helps you to find the information you want.

One of the best places to start is:

www.google.com

In the search box you can type in what you are interested in and click 'search'. For example, if you are studying biology and you need to write an assignment on cell differentiation then you could type in 'cell differentiation'.

However, if you don't know exactly what you are looking for, it may be better to use a search engine like the following:

www.yahoo.com

Again there is a search box, but there are also many choices below it. If you know that you are looking for something about science, then click on that category. On the next screen you will see a list of scientific topics like those shown in Figure 7. You can then choose the next level, and so on, until you find what you want.

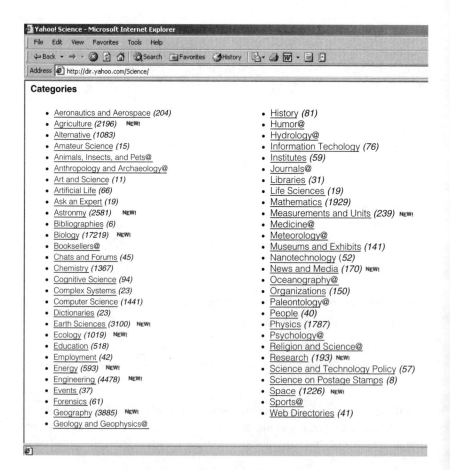

Figure 7   List of scientific topics

Local search engines are found only in a certain country or a certain region. They help you find sites in or about that country more easily, and let you search in your own language.

Yahoo, for example, has many local sites, such as:

asia.yahoo.com

For the whole of Asia.

www.yahoo.com/r/cc

For China.

Finding information in your own language certainly helps your understanding. However, there is a problem when you want to quote that source in an assignment. Unless you are writing for one of the languages departments, you will, of course, have to quote in English so that the marker can understand it.

Search tips
Here are some ways of making your search easy.

1. First of all make your search as specific/detailed/exact as possible.
The more general your search is, the more sites you will find. For example, if we search for 'biology' in Google, we find 6,770,000 sites! If we search for 'cell biology' we find 542,000. That is still a big number but only about 8% of our previous search. If we search for 'cell biology in China' we find 12 sites.

2. The trick in finding the right sites is knowing how to search.
Many search engines have an 'advanced search' page where you can make your search much more specific. Let's have a look at Yahoo's advanced search page in Figure 8. Now look at the details. It will probably help you if you read this as you sit at the screen looking at the actual website. In the first part you see the words 'Show results with', and a choice of phrases, as listed in Table 14.

Some of the other options are quite advanced but a few of them are very useful. For example, if you want to, you can search for websites only in your own language.

You can also search by domain name, such as .com or .org. Why is this useful? Well, suppose you want to find information about a topic related to

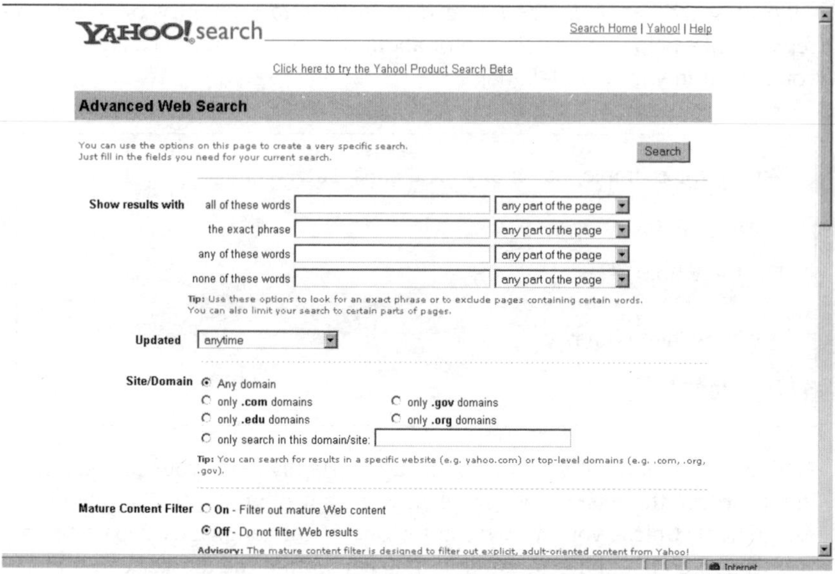

Figure 8   Yahoo's advanced search page

a certain country and you know the domain name for that country (e.g. '.jp' for Japan, '.kr' for Korea). Then you can use this option. Also, if you don't want commercial information (shops) but only academic information, then use .ac (short for 'academic') or use .org (short for 'organisation').

▶ Ways of reading

For the last part of this chapter we look at different ways of reading. As you know from your first language, we do not read all types of writing the same way. Think about the difference between reading a letter from a friend and reading letters in the daily newspaper. Reading them for different purposes means reading them in different ways. Here are some of those ways.

Scanning

Scanning is a fast way of reading to find something you want. Scanning an article or a chapter is a bit like the way a bird flies over a garden looking for

Table 14 Commands for finding websites

Phrase	Meaning
all of these words	means that if you search for 'cell biology in China' you will find a site that somewhere on its pages has the words 'cell', 'biology', 'in' and 'China'.
the exact phrase	will only show results when it finds exactly what you typed in. This usually gives you good results.
any of the words	is useful if you are looking for a number of very specific terms. If you are interested in sites with information about any of these words then use this option.
None of these words	If you are looking for information on computers but not for shops, you could search for 'computers' and use 'without the words' . . . 'shops', 'buy'.

bits of food. The bird's eye is looking for one thing such as a worm and when it sees the worm, down it flies. It takes no notice of all the leaves and flowers. In the same way, you can scan the article for a particular word or phrase.

You already know how to scan. You do it every time you look up a name in the telephone book or let your eye go down the page of a newspaper to find a word or phrase you are interested in. Do the same thing with your university reading. Decide what the key words are that interest you. For example, if you are interested in the topic of migration and you want to know if an article mentions reasons for migration, and 'push and pull' factors in particular, then make your eye scan quickly down the page to find the words 'push' and 'pull'. If those words appear a few times, then the article is probably worth reading in more detail. If not, go to the next article.

Skimming

Skimming is like looking right through someone else's holiday photograph album quickly. You want to get a general idea of where they went and what they did but you don't need to understand and remember every detail.

When you skim through an article you are looking for the big picture to answer questions like these:

* *What is this topic about?*
* *What are the main ideas here?*

(As well as skimming, you can also go to the first sentence in each paragraph to find the topics.)

Using the index
On the other hand, if you are trying to understand something difficult which you have heard or will soon hear in a lecture, then you need to take more time. Look in the index of the recommended book and follow up each reference.

Reading efficiently
Once you have found the right place in the book or found the right article, then start reading. Here are some suggestions.

1.   Read word groups
Can you remember when you learned to read your own language as a child? At first you read one word and another word and another word very slowly. For faster reading look at word groups. Try to make your eye move quickly along the row instead of reading each word separately:

    NO: All – experiments – need – to – be
    YES: All experiments – need to be

If you are a quick reader in your own language then you know what to do. If you are a slow reader, now is the time to go faster. If you find this difficult, look for a Speed Reading course at your university's Student Learning Centre.

2.   Think ahead
After you have read the title, stop and ask yourself:

- *What will this chapter be about?*
- *What questions will it answer?*

After you have read the first sentence in a paragraph stop and say to yourself:

- *What will come next?*
- *Where will the examples come from?*

3.   Ask yourself, 'What do I know already?'
As you start reading, remind yourself of all that you know already about this subject. For example, if you are studying the topic of human genes

for a course in biology then you probably know already that DNA contains information.

Some people think reading goes just one way:

the book → the reader

Most often, reading goes two ways:

the book ↔ the reader

In other words, as you read you are reminding yourself of facts you know already. If you are reading a history book and see the phrase 'Europe in the early 1920s' you say to yourself, 'Oh yes, World War I had just finished then.'

4. Look at the link words

Link words join ideas. As well as the new subject words you will meet in your university study, there are also very important link (or joining) words that are the same for all subjects. In Table 15 there are some to look out for. There are many more.

Table 15 Words to join ideas

Link words	Meaning	The words join
in addition	and	two equal ideas
on the other hand however	but	two opposite ideas
provided that	if	a condition
given that since	because	a fact and a reason
despite the fact that	even though	two opposites
although	even though	two opposites
similarly	in the same way	two ideas or findings
on the contrary	the opposite	two opposites
as opposed to	the opposite	two opposites
rather than	not	two different ideas

Talk about your reading with other students

Reading is one thing; understanding what you read is another. In many courses students work together after class to prepare for writing assignments. Talking about your reading is one way of preparing. Here is how one group worked together.

> In our reading group we had six people. We tried two ideas. One was for everyone to read a different article and then report on it. That was OK but not really good because sometimes the reader didn't understand something and then nobody understood it. We changed our plan. We made two copies of each chapter or article. Then for about 10 minutes two people talked together about their article. Then we took turns to 'teach' the others in the group.
>
> We made a rule. Nobody should read aloud from the article. They should say it in their own words. That way we could understand it better. We had questions after each article. At the end of one hour we all had a good idea about 3 articles.

► Recognising word parts

Most of the time the best way to understand the meaning of a new word is to read the whole sentence and think of its meaning, as explained in Chapter 3. Reading the whole paragraph is an even better way of working out word meanings. However, for many academic words, if you know something about word parts you can sometimes work out the meaning of quite technical terms.

Word beginnings and endings (prefixes and suffixes)

As well as working out a word's meaning from the words around it or by going to the dictionary, looking at the parts of the word sometimes helps. Many words in English are made up from parts of other languages. In the language of study many of these are from Latin and Greek. As you read many of these you will start to recognise the same parts in different words.

We call the first part of a word a *prefix* if it has its own meaning. In English most of our prefixes come from the ancient Greek or Latin languages. In Table 16 you can see just a few of the many prefixes you will meet in English words.

Table 16   Word beginnings (prefixes)

Prefix	English meaning	Example
ante- & pre-	= before	pre-war = before the war
anti-	= against	anti-war protestors
inter-	= between	interaction = action between people
intra-	= inside	intravenous = inside the veins
mis-	= wrong	misinterpreting = interpreting the wrong way
multi-	= many	multinational = for many nations
neo-	= new	neo-colonialism = new colonising
pan-	= all	pan-Pacific = all the Pacific, throughout the Pacific
post-	= after	post-war = after the war
tele-	= far away	telephone = hear from far away

The last part of a word is called a *suffix* if it has a meaning of its own. Suffixes can also tell you what part of speech the word is. Table 17 has just two nouns (N) and two adjectives (A) to give you the idea.

Table 17   Word endings (suffixes)

Suffix	Meaning	Example
-ance, ence (N)	state of being	residence, permanence
-age (N)	belonging to	percentage, coverage
-ful (A)	with	doubtful, meaningful
-less (A)	without	doubtless, purposeless

Other word parts

As well as prefixes and suffixes you can find parts of Greek and Latin words in other parts of English words. It is worth learning the meaning of some common examples. For example, *demos* is the word for 'people' and *crat* or '*cratic*' means 'to govern', to 'rule', or to have 'power'. Therefore a 'democratic' government is a system where the people in the country have the power. In other words, all adult citizens can vote. In Table 18 there are just three more of many examples from Greek.

Table 18 Greek compound words

Greek	Greek	English word	Meaning of English word
auto = self, alone	*cratic* = to govern	an autocrat	a person who rules a country alone
graph = words, writing	*mono* = one	a monograph	a text written by one person
poly = many	*glot* = tongue, language	a polyglot	someone who speaks many languages

From Latin we have another set of words. There are just two examples in Table 19.

Table 19 Word parts from Latin

Latin	Latin	English word	Meaning
multi = many	*media* = methods	multimedia	using many methods of communicating
inter = between	*venire* = to come	intervene	come between two or more people/countries etc.

As we have seen, knowing the parts of words, whatever language they come from, can sometimes help you with working out meaning. English has some words where all the parts are made up of other words. These are called 'compound words'. That is, each part of the word has meaning and together the parts make a meaning of their own. The following compound words and their parts are taken from the Macquarie dictionary.

biomedicine = concerned with the effect of the environment on the human body
brain-dead = having no further electrical activity in the brain

However, even without the dictionary you could probably have worked out the meaning of the first word if you knew that *bio* = life.

In this chapter we have shown you ways to make your reading not just faster but also better. Have you found out anything new? If you are already a good reader in your first language you could be thinking, 'I do that anyway.' Then all you need to do is to use those good skills you already have to be a successful reader in your new language. Perhaps, too, you are already well used to using the Internet for other purposes. Now you can make use of your ability for your university studies.

If you would like to read more on this topic, many books have been written to help you. One is a guide in the Palgrave Study Skills Series by Nicholas Marsh, called *How to Begin Studying English Literature*. You can find more information about this on the following website: www.palgrave.com.

7 Assignments and Examinations

Many books have been written to help students write better university assignments, especially essays. Three of these titles are listed at the end of this chapter. However, essays are only one type of university writing and different departments have different types of assignment. For example, in a practical programme such as Dentistry your assignments could include notes you take while working with patients, which you then write as a case study. In Education you could be doing a survey, which you then write as a report. In this chapter we describe some different types of university writing and how to write them well. The advice comes from what teachers and students have told us.

This chapter answers the following questions:

- What are some common writing problems of university students?
- What different types of assignment do lecturers set?
- How can students understand the assignment question?
- What can good writers teach others?
- In how many ways can students have feedback on their writing?

▶ Common problems

Teachers who mark assignments say that the same problems appear time and time again. They also say that many of these problems are the same for all students, whether they speak English as their first or second language and whether they are studying engineering or computer science, history or business. Here are three common problems. (A fourth problem, not understanding the question, is discussed later in the chapter.)

The 'mechanics' of writing
The 'mechanics' of writing are punctuation, spelling and sentence structure. Punctuation in writing does the same job as the tone of the voice does in

talking. It helps to make reading (or listening) easier. One way to see whether your punctuation is right is to try reading your writing aloud to yourself. If your spoken English is quite good you will stop naturally where there should be full stops, pause where there should be commas and raise your voice at the end of a sentence that needs a question mark.

Don't blame yourself if you are not a strong speller. English has many strange spellings which go back a long way in the history of the language. Spelling is a major problem for some students, while others seem able to look at a word they have written and say immediately 'That's wrong.' One thing that makes words start to look right or wrong to you is that you have seen them in print often. That's another reason for doing plenty of reading!

You can learn a few rules, such as this one to help you with the spelling of words like *believe* and *receipt*:

If it rhymes with 'SEE'
Put I before E
Except after C.

The first line reminds you that the rule is only for words rhyming with 'see', not for words like 'height'. The second and third lines tell you the rule. However, rules don't cover everything. If you don't know a rule, sometimes pronunciation helps. Try saying the difficult word aloud.

Another way to remove spelling mistakes is the Spellcheck on your computer, which helps by highlighting words it thinks are wrong and letting you know other possible spellings. However, that doesn't always help either, especially in university writing when the computer doesn't recognise technical words in your subject.

A third part of the 'mechanics' of writing is sentence structure. What is a sentence and what is not? Essay markers say that the two most common mistakes here are:

- putting a full stop after words that aren't a sentence;
- not putting enough full stops.

Later in the chapter, under the heading 'Advice from students', there are suggestions for improving the mechanics of your writing.

Organisation

Another major problem is organising the ideas. Whether you are writing an essay or a report, the way you put the information together makes reading easier or more difficult for the reader, who is usually the person giving you your grades. As we'll see later in this chapter, you can learn about the patterns for some types of writing but in the end no two pieces of work follow exactly the same plan. Everyone in the class may have the same essay topic but they will all have their own way of organising the ideas.

Computers are both a help and a problem for organising your writing. Before computers were common, students would write out their work, leave it for a day or two and then read it through and perhaps change the order of some things. That meant taking a long time to copy out the whole essay again. Now, computers make it so easy to pick paragraphs up and put them in different places that we have a different problem. When a paragraph is moved from near the start to near the end, the flow of the whole piece of writing also changes. The writer has to leave time to reread it and decide whether the whole work still flows smoothly after being moved around.

Words

Student writers have two main problems with the words they choose for their writing. One is that they don't have enough words to say what they mean, and the other is that they don't always use the right word in the right place. (You have already read about ways of building up your vocabulary in Chapter 3.) Solving the other problem, not knowing which word is best where, takes longer. As we saw with spelling, the more you read, the better you become at putting the right word in the right place.

Summary of problems

One way to answer the question 'What makes a good essay?' is to say that writing an essay is like making a cake. To be successful, a cake needs to have all the ingredients, not just some. It's no good having the eggs and the flour but forgetting to add the liquid. In an essay the ingredients are:

ideas + words + organisation

You need all three to have a good essay.

Unless you are a postgraduate student doing original work, nobody expects to find really new ideas in your essays. Your ideas come from reading and from listening to lectures. As we saw in Chapter 4, lecture notes are important because they give you the big picture for your essay topics, but they are not the whole story. As one student from China said,

At first I didn't understand what sort of essay the lecturers wanted. I thought the best thing was to give back all the things the lecturer had said. That was wrong. I was supposed to do more reading myself. Once I understood that, my essays had better marks.

Another way of collecting ideas is at tutorials, where the tutor will lead discussions, usually about topics that will be covered in your essays (see Chapter 5). These discussions needn't finish at the end of the tutorial. Informal out-of-class discussions are helpful too.

Once you have collected the ideas, you need to find the best words to express them. The words come partly from books and partly from your own vocabulary, which you are gradually building up. As you read for a particular assignment you will be writing down words and phrases to use in your essay. However, read what is said about plagiarism, below.

We have also discussed the organisation of the essay. There are many different ways to organise your ideas. Three writers with the same material could organise their essays in three different ways. For example, here are two patterns.

1. Theory, theory, theory. Examples, examples, examples.
2. Theory, examples, theory, examples, theory, examples.

In the end, what is important is that it is easy to read. That is why students often give their essays to someone else to read.

▶ Plagiarism

We come now to a topic that is very serious at universities: plagiarism. Here is a definition of plagiarism.

Plagiarism = using others' ideas and words without clearly
acknowledging the source of that information

To give you a good example, read the last sentence again. We wrote it without telling you that this is not our own definition. It was copied from a website: www.indiana.edu/~wts/wts/plagiarism.html

Now that we have told you that someone else wrote the sentence, it is not plagiarised any more.

Many students nowadays look on the Internet for material for their assignments and are tempted to copy something they find. Some students even send their papers to each other, and there are even websites that help students do this. This is also plagiarism.

Let's look at another example. Read the following passage by a student in Asian history.

> The Industrial Revolution held out the prospect of a reciprocal trade, in which the counterpart of the export of agricultural and mineral products from Southeast Asia would be the importation of the manufactures of Europe. However, . . .

These are actually not the student's words. He copied them from a book called *Southeast Asia: A Modern History*, by Nicholas Tarling. We call this 'plagiarism' because the student did not tell us that the sentence was not his own. Have a look at the paragraph below.

> It looked as if the Industrial Revolution could help Southeast Asia to export agricultural and mineral products in return for imports from Europe.

This is also a type of plagiarism. As you can see, the student took the ideas from the same book and rewrote them. The words are different but the ideas are not. Unfortunately, again he did not tell us that these were not his ideas. Now look at the paragraph below.

> . . . about this period we read: 'The Industrial Revolution held out the prospect of a reciprocal trade, in which the counterpart of the export of agricultural and mineral products from Southeast Asia would be the importation of the manufactures of Europe. However . . .' (Tarling, 2001).

Here the student has shown us that the part marked ('. . .') comes from somewhere else. He has shown that the ideas are not his own in three ways:

1. By saying 'we read'.
2. By using quotation marks ('. . .') around the author's words.
3. By naming the author and the date it was published: (Tarling, 2001).

The words 'Tarling, 2001' are called the *reference*. You don't use full references in the text but you do give details, either as a footnote or at the end of your assignment.

Another way of referring to other people's ideas is to paraphrase, like this.

> Tarling (2001) writes that it looked as if the Industrial Revolution could help Southeast Asia to export agricultural and mineral products in return for imports from Europe.

As you can see, this is the same text as the second example above, but the student has now added 'Tarling writes that . . .', making it clear that the information in the following words comes from someone else. He has written down the author's ideas, using his own words. As you see, you don't use quotation marks for paraphrasing.

So when do you *not* have to quote or reference?

(a) You are not plagiarising when you write your own words *and* your own ideas. For example, when you write a poem or a short story, that is your own work because the ideas and the words are yours.

(b) You are not plagiarising when you write the result of an experiment you have done. For example, when you do an experiment for your study, then you can write about the results without referencing because you found the results by yourself.

(c) You are not plagiarising when you describe something you have experienced, or something you feel or think, and you use your own words. For example, at the end of an essay you might write:

> It seems that researchers do not agree about . . . Perhaps further evidence will come soon to show. . . .

Here the student's words show that he or she has read work about the same topic by different authors. The student has compared other people's ideas, looked at the facts, checked them, thought about them, and then come to a conclusion. Because that conclusion is the student's own idea, there is no need to reference the other works which have already appeared in the essay.

How serious is plagiarism?

Plagiarising is a very serious offence. In fact it is so serious that in many universities you will lose your marks for the course concerned, and maybe even get suspended (sent away) from the university.

If you are reading other students' papers to get ideas, of course that is fine, but be careful not to make the mistake of using their work as your own.

There are websites that help lecturers find out if a text is original or plagiarized, such as:

www.turnitin.com

Another example is

www.plagiarism.com

▶ Types of assignment

In this section we discuss three types of assignment: essays, responding to case studies, and reports. Essays are common in the Arts and Social Sciences, while science and mathematics subjects and professional degrees such as Engineering have different types of assignment, such as reports. For information about your own subject, see the departmental handbook. The advice in this section is about five common types of university assignment.

Expository essays

In expository essays you report things which other people have said. Here is an example of an expository essay topic:

> Assess the impact of the Reform Bill of 1832 on the working class in Britain.

Look in the library or on your course website to see more examples of topics.

To prepare for writing an expository essay you read from as many sources as possible and summarise them all in your own words and with a few quotations. As we discussed under 'Plagiarism' you must reference (name) all your sources in the text and in a proper list at the end. Table 20 has some things you do and do not do in an expository essay.

Table 20 Writing an expository essay

Don't	Do
Summarise each article one after the other.	Put together all the ideas on the same topic from several articles.
Write as if your essay was a list.	Link your ideas within paragraphs and from one paragraph to the next.
Pretend you are the author of other people's ideas.	List all the authors of work you refer to.
Write only what you heard in lectures.	Read as widely as possible.

Argument essays

An argument essay looks at two or more sides of a question. You tell the reader different opinions from various writers on the same topic and then reach some sort of conclusion. Here are two examples of argument essays:

The Industrial Revolution was not at all revolutionary. Discuss.

Assess the arguments made by opponents of capitalism in eighteenth-century America.

In argument essays students don't have to say 'This one is right . . .' but they do make statements like these:

It seems that . . .

X makes a strong argument for . . . while *Y*'s case seems . . .

As with the expository essay, from your reading you will find words you can use directly (quotations) and ideas you can put in your own words (paraphrasing). These help to make your essay stronger. Because you also write the source of these ideas, you are showing the lecturer that you are reading widely.

Analytical essays

To write an analytical essay you have to look in close detail at something. Analytical essays are important in subjects like Fine Arts, Literature and Film Studies. Here is an example of an essay topic from a drama course:

Write a close analysis of one of the designated scenes or sequences from . . .

Here are some steps you could take to write an analytical essay on this topic.

1. Borrow the video from the film library and find the scenes they refer to.
2. Decide which scene you would like to write about.
3. Play it over several times, looking at the details and taking notes.
4. Look at any list of suggestions you have had in class or on the assignment sheet. Try to find examples of these in the video.
5. As you write the essay look carefully at any instructions you have been given about the essay length and so on.

Responding to case studies

A case study is an example, usually from real life, of some theory you are studying. The assignment asks you to talk about (study) the example (case). Here is one case study question:

You are the adviser to . . . Your clients have asked you to tell them the best way of. . . .

(a) Outline three possible courses of action.
(b) Mention which you would take and give reasons.

To answer the question, you need to do more than just give your own ideas. You need to refer to your reading. The words 'give reasons' usually mean reasons that have been set out by others.

Reports

A report tells what you (and perhaps a group of other students) have done. In subjects like engineering or science, assignments include reports on work such as:

an experiment;
working with a client;
interviews;
observing things, animals or people.

To write the report you have to collect new material, either by yourself or with other students. Each subject has quite clear ways of setting out a report and you need to find out what these are in your subject. For example, a book written for science students, which is listed at the end of this chapter, includes report writing.

▶ Understanding the assignment

Whatever type of assignment you have, it is easy to look at the question quickly and then start writing it. To be certain that your work is on the right topic, take time first to understand exactly what is being asked.

Why is it so difficult to understand the questions?

Some students say 'I can understand all the questions they ask me in class so why can't I understand assignment questions?' One reason is because of differences in spoken and written language, as we see in the following examples, one asked in class and the other a written examination question. The meaning of both is the same.

Class question:

Can you tell me what happened in the field of second language motivation research about ten years ago?

Examination question:
Describe the change in second language motivational research that took place in the early 1990s. Describe where the impetus for this change came from and the effect this change has had on subsequent research. List the names of people or publications that were important to this change.

Notice some differences between the two questions, as summarised in Table 21.

Table 21 Differences between spoken and written questions

Spoken questions	Examination questions
Use 'you'.	Don't address a person.
Start with 'Can you?' or a 'question word' (who, why, etc.).	Start with a verb: 'describe', 'compare', 'list', etc.
Ask one question at a time.	Have 4 questions in one: 'describe the change', 'describe where . . .', 'describe the effect' and 'list the names'.

The language of assignment and examination questions
Whether you are writing essays for assignments or for examinations, the first step is to think about what the language of the question actually means. Here are some examples of how questions start.

- Discuss the role of . . .
- Give an account of . . .
- Explain/Discuss the reasons for . . .

Because most essays are questions even though they don't have a 'question word', you could try and turn the sentence into a question starting with How? Why? What if? In Table 22 we show how some essay topics can be changed into spoken questions so you can understand exactly what they are asking.

Answering the question
Now let's compare two answers to the class question at the beginning of this section. To answer the question in class, a student might say:

Researchers started using second language theory more to explain motivation in second language learning, rather than general psychology.

Table 22   What essay topics mean

The essay asks . . .	A spoken question asks . . .
1. Discuss the role of . . .	What is the purpose of . . . ?
2. Give an account of . . .	What happened . . . ?
3. Explain/Discuss the reasons for . . .	Why did . . . happen? What caused . . . ?
4. Discuss the significance of . . .	Why is . . . important?
5. Distinguish between . . .	What is the difference between . . . ?
6. Account for . . .	Why . . . ?
7. Describe the characteristics of . . .	What is . . . like?
8. Make the case for . . .	Why should . . . ?
9. Draw some parallels between . . .	What is similar about . . . ?
10. Outline the effects of . . .	What was the result of . . . ?

However, in an examination answer the same student might write something like this:

> During the early 1990s a paradigm-shift occurred in the field of second language motivation research. It was found that the specific characteristics of second language learning compared with other forms of learning warranted a new strand of research. Researchers involved in the investigation of motivation in classroom learning found strong relationships between the educational setting and learner motivation. This to them meant that specific attention had to be given to the educational context as well as the application of research findings in classroom teaching. An article by Crookes and Schmidt in 1991 was the first to explicitly address these issues and a subsequent debate in the *Modern Language Journal* in 1994 also has been very influential.

1. **Say everything**
   In a class or tutorial, when the lecturer or tutor asks a question, you give a short answer, but then you have a chance to add more information if the questioner says 'What exactly do you mean by that?' or 'Can you give us an example?' When you write an answer in an assignment, on the other hand, you have to say everything at once.

2. **Answer the exact question**

As we have seen, essay questions may start with any one of a number of different words. You need to look at these carefully. When you describe something you say *what* the thing is like. When you explain something you say *why*, using words like 'because', 'the reason' etc. For example:

Because of the force of . . .

The reason/explanation for this is . . .

▶ Advice from students

We asked some university students who spoke English as a second language and who had very good essay grades to tell us why they were doing so well. Here is what they said.

Attend a workshop

One student attended a weekly workshop at a Student Learning Centre for a semester to collect ideas about writing assignments.

I learned some techniques and methods from a writing workshop at the Student Learning Centre. Now I get better grades for my assignments. One thing they showed us was how to think about exactly why we were writing each sentence in the introduction.

One writing workshop was about the purpose of the introduction to an essay. They used the example of an expository essay with the title 'Strategies for learning English' and they showed the students how each sentence in the introduction has a purpose, like this.

The introduction	The purpose of the sentence
Because of computer technology and globalisation of many major industries, English has become an important world language. For this reason thousands of students come to stay in English-speaking countries in order to learn the	• gives background to the essay topic • adds more to the background

Continued

language as an investment for the future. However, some students become frustrated by their slow progress in the early stages. This problem could be eased by using effective strategies for acquiring English. Language learning strategies can be broken into four main categories: environment, the four skills (reading, listening, writing and speaking), vocabulary and attitude. This essay is aimed at intermediate or upper level students and discusses these areas in some depth.	• states a problem • mentions the essay topic • gives the essay sub-topics • states the essay focus

Workshops may be organised by your department or by the Student Learning Centre. Some could be free (paid for out of your fees) but others may have to be paid for as an extra. At Student Learning Centre workshops you will meet students from many different departments, and both new and native speakers of English.

Talk with the lecturer about your draft copies
A few staff are willing to read the drafts of your assignment, particularly if you are a senior student or in a small class. Then they might write comments on the draft or ask you to come and discuss it. Usually these comments will be about the content of the essay rather than the language.

Practise writing
Some people who find writing a difficult task do as little writing as possible. Unfortunately this makes it difficult to improve. By contrast, students who enjoy writing usually write more, and therefore get even better. As this student says, not all the writing you do need be for assignments.

I enjoy writing. Sometimes I write things even when I don't have to.

Write first, revise later
Try to keep writing your ideas in the assignment for as long as you can, using whatever words come to mind, without worrying too much about the language. Then you can go back later and improve the vocabulary and the organisation. As one student said:

My words don't stop my thinking.

Learn from good writers

Students can learn how to write better if they see good examples of essays, as this student found.

> *I read aloud from good essays. That way I can hear good language in my head.*

Finding 'good' assignments is not as easy as it sounds. Some students, like this next one, told us that it was difficult to find examples.

> *Why can't we see the good essays with the A+ grades? The other students won't let you see their essays.*

This is a common problem. How can you see the marked essays of other students when teachers cannot copy a student's essay and hand it out to others? Talk to your class representative to see if one or two class members who have done really well will let other people see photocopies of their essays.

When you look at an essay that has a high grade, remember to read the comments from the marker. They should explain why this essay had such a good mark. Has the marker made any suggestions for making it better? Even an essay with a high grade could improve. Some people say you should look too at the essays with the low grades to see the difference. What does the marker say is wrong?

Talk about essay writing

This next student has a good idea.

> *I go round asking other people for advice. Sometimes they'll tell you how they prepared to write the essay and that's even better than seeing their actual essay. When I look at a good essay I just think 'I could never be that good,' but when they tell me how they got there I think I could do that.*

If you talk about essay writing with all the students in your class you will collect plenty of ideas to try with your next essay.

Use the computer to improve your writing

When you are writing essays or assignments, the computer can be a great help. Wordprocessing software like Microsoft® Word® or Corel® Wordperfect® have functions that can make the writing process easier. One is the Spellchecker, a function that many people are familiar with and use frequently. This can check not only spelling but also grammar. If you make a mistake, or the Spellchecker doesn't recognise a word you wrote, then it will make suggestions. Recent versions of these programs also have a built-in *thesaurus* that gives you synonyms of words you have used. That means you needn't use the same word six times in one paragraph.

If you have used some words too often (for example twice in the same sentence) or if you have used the wrong word by mistake right through your essay, you can use the Find function and automatically replace all the found words with another one.

Another useful feature of many word processors is the Word Count function, which will tell you how many pages, words and even characters your document has. This is great for seeing how far you are with your assignment when you are aiming for a certain number of words. You can also select just part of the text, and the Word Count function will tell you how long parts of your document are, such as the introduction, or the conclusion.

The computer is excellent for joint projects, that is, for assignments where you are working with other students. For example, this book has two authors. As we write, we both add to the document, comment on and edit each other's additions and then send these back to the other author. This paragraph is being written by one of us, but the other one will soon be checking it, commenting on it and maybe changing it. Students often have to do the same thing when they do assignments in groups. How do you exchange information? Many word processors allow you to underline, colour, or highlight text so that it stands out from the rest of the text. They also let you insert comments that are not part of the text but make a comment about the text. Later versions of word processors have tracking functions that show additions made by several authors in different colours and let you see which parts of the text have been changed. Since all word processing programs are different it is best to read the Help files to find out exactly how to do this.

There are many good dictionaries available on CD roms and even DVDs, but if you have access to the Internet, there are also many free online dictionaries you can access.

One of the best ones is:

www.macmillaneducation.com/catalogue/dictionaries/med.htm

This dictionary by Macmillan is very large but is easy to understand because it only uses 2500 words to explain the meaning of all the words and phrases.

If you have access to the internet, there are also many free online dictionaries you can access.

Here are some good ones to start with:

www.dictionary.com

There is also a thesaurus:

www.thesaurus.com

If your first language is Chinese, Japanese or Korean and you know Pinyin, then you can use this online dictionary to find an English translation:

www.chinalanguage.com/CCDICT/index.html

The following dictionary is a special one. You download the program onto your computer and download dictionaries. Then, when you are using your word processor or even when you are reading any other text on your computer (such as a website), you can click on any word and get a translation.

www.babylon.com

Learn from textbooks

Some students find that having a textbook about academic writing is a help, even if they don't attend an actual writing class. You may even be able to find a book that tells you about essay writing in your own subject. This is how one student used a writing textbook.

I bought myself a textbook on essay writing and then I used it in various ways like trying out the exercises and then looking up the answers.

This is one way of doing a textbook exercise. Here are someone's planning notes for an essay on the topic 'Language learners can help themselves'. The points are written down just as the student thought of them, with main headings and smaller points all mixed up. Photocopy the box below and cut it up. Then try putting the parts into order. Which would be good headings? Which points could go under each heading?

Topic: Language learners can help themselves

Introduction

Range of informal and formal opportunities

Reasons for self-help

Announcement of essay plan

Finding the right level of class

Listening to the radio

Informal learning opportunities

Examples of informal opportunities

Ways of learning informally

Finding opportunities to talk

Problems and overcoming them

Shortage of time

Time management

Making the most of class time

Shyness

Formal learning opportunities

Choosing the right course

Using textbooks out of class

Comparison of formal and informal learning

Conclusion

Summary of learners' roles

Encouragement to get started

Test yourself
There is not just one answer to this exercise. Try doing it with some friends and talk about different possible ways of organising the plan you had, before looking at the end of the chapter for one suggestion.

► Students' questions about assignments

This next section is a collection of questions often asked by students about their university assignments.

What does 'tone' mean?

The marker said last time that the tone of my essay needed improving. What does that mean?

It's not easy to answer this question without looking at the actual essay, but here are a couple of common problems. One is that student writers sometimes bring themselves into an essay too much by using 'I' quite often, like this:

I think . . .

I believe . . .

The short answer is 'Don't do this.' Even if you have done original work, the practice in university writing is to leave yourself out of the picture, like this:

It seems as if . . .

These findings suggest . . .

In summary, it is probably the case that . . .

When you read research reports in scientific fields such as physics and mathematics you will see that the writers do not say:

I found that if you take some of X and some of Y, you get . . .

But rather:

The results indicate that combining X and Y results in . . .

This is not a definite rule for all types of academic writing. Other research fields, such as some areas of psychology, do use the pronoun 'I' because their kind of research is different. Psychology often deals with people and their experiences, making it hard for the research to stay completely objective. You can find statements such as:

When investigating this classroom, I could feel the tension rising as soon as . . .

Another problem is related to this one. Academic writers try not to be too definite. The result may sound as if they are a bit unsure about their findings, but that is the style. Here is an example:

Although the results point in this direction, it is not entirely certain if . . .

This practice is called 'hedging'. Again, the best advice is to read as much as you can in your area to get a good idea of what is the common tone or style.

Can I write the way we were taught to write in my country?

Different cultures write in different ways. In order to be successful in the university where you are now studying, you need to follow their style. If you have never studied at a university in your own country, then this may not be a problem to you. You will be learning new ways of writing just as native speakers of English do when they start university.

Here is one example of differences in writing traditions. In Western cultures many reports and research articles start with the topic of the text.

This article will report on a study of the smoking habits of teenagers in the Netherlands . . .

By contrast, in many Asian cultures announcing the topic often comes later. This means that when English speakers go to university in, say, China or Korea, they have to learn new ways of writing. Similarly students from China, Korea and other Asian countries have to find out about new ways of putting reports together.

These differences are not just between Asian and Western countries. There are also many differences in the way people write between one European language and another. Spanish writers use far fewer explanations of what they mean than British writers. Even within English-speaking cultures there are differences. In British research articles, for example, there is more often an abstract of the article than in American research articles. American articles also use fewer definitions and statistical examples than British articles.

You will need to learn what is done in the country where you choose to study.

What's the difference between a good and a not so good essay?

Students often ask this, especially if their mark is not as high as they would like. We asked some teachers to give a short answer to the question and here is what they said.

- It's the difference between keeping to the topic or going off the topic.
- A 'not so good' essay has very few references. The student has read maybe just one or two books.
- A good essay is well organised. In a weak essay the facts may be there but the reader has to look carefully for them.
- The difference between a good essay and the others is that the good one follows the instructions about word length and so on.

How do I join my ideas up? I have lots of things to say but they are like a list.

Yes, this is a problem. Joining your ideas means much more than putting 'and . . . and . . . and' in your essay. Some people make the mistake of throwing in a whole lot of 'joining' words without checking to see if the ideas really flow on from one another. Other people make the opposite mistake. They have the ideas in a sensible order but the reader has to find this out without the writer's help because there are no joining words. You will find more about essay writing in the books listed at the end of this chapter.

How do other people check for accuracy? I read my essay over at the end but I never find my mistakes.

Here are some suggestions for checking the final copy of your essay.

- Ask a native speaker of English to read it just for the language, not for the content.
- Before your final check, leave it for a while and then come back to it.
- Use the spellchecker on your computer.

How can I take time writing when we have so many assignments?

Have you heard the story of the hare and the tortoise (turtle)? They were taking part in a race and everyone thought that of course the hare, being a fast runner, would win while the tortoise crawled slowly along. In fact, the tortoise was the winner because he just kept on moving whereas the hare, with the long legs, was always stopping for a rest. Like the hare you mustn't take so many breaks that you miss the date for handing in the essay – although some breaks are a good idea: they give you time to think about the essay rather than just handing in the first thing you have written. However, like the tortoise, even if you are a slow writer you need to keep going. The story of the hare and tortoise ends with a saying that could describe successful essay writers, 'Slow and steady wins the race.'

Summary of advice

Here is a summary of advice about how to be a good essay writer.

1. Look at good essays written by other students, after they are marked.
2. Read the guidelines from your department on how to present an essay.
3. Attend classes or workshops on essay writing.
4. Talk with the marker about your own problem. Here is one conversation between a teacher and student.

Teacher: Listen while I read aloud from one of your sentences ('. . .'). What's the problem?

Student: The sentence is rather long.

Teacher: Yes. In fact it goes for one-third of a page. Do you think that matters?

Student: In my school they told us that long sentences were better than short sentences.

Teacher: These things go in and out of fashion. In the end, what do you think matters?

Student: It should make sense.

Teacher: Let me show you how we could have better sense here by breaking the ideas down into smaller units.

The lecturer then showed the student how to improve that part of the essay.

▶ The teacher's feedback

When your essay is returned to you the lecturer will usually give you some feedback, which answers questions like these:

How good is this essay?

Have I done what the lecturer wanted?

Which parts could be improved?

Feedback includes the grades, the marks and the comments which the teacher writes about your essay. Later in the chapter you will find out about getting feedback from your fellow students and about giving yourself some feedback. Now here is some information about grades, marks and written comments.

Grades and marks

An essay might have a grade (say B+) and/or a mark such as 55% or 50/80. Marks are like grades but more detailed. Departments sometimes give you a list explaining what mark equals what grade and how much you need for a pass, but in general pass grades go from A+ to C–. The grade of D+ or lower is certainly a fail but in some departments C– is also a fail. Your department handbook should give you this information.

When students receive their grades, some are very excited because they didn't realise they were so good, while others rush to ask the lecturer why their mark is so low. This can happen even if the grade is average, such as a B. Students who have changed countries to go to university sometimes get a big shock when they find that their essay marks are not always A grades. As one student said:

This B grade is shameful. I always had an A in my country and my parents spent a lot of money sending me here. I don't know which points I missed out to get such a low grade.

Before you feel too worried try and find out what grades others have got. That's not easy because the staff are not allowed to tell you other students' marks and some students are not happy to talk about their results. If you are really concerned about your mark, make an appointment to discuss the problem. See Chapter 9 for ways of contacting the lecturer.

Written comments

In small classes your essay will probably be marked by the lecturer you know, but in large classes tutors may do the marking. Whoever the marker is, usually there will be individual comments on each essay. The advantage of this is that the comments are written just for you. The disadvantage could be that you can't read the marker's handwriting.

What has the marker said and not said?

In reading the comments, keep in mind that markers do not like to be unkind when they believe a student has tried hard. Because of this you may need to 'read between the lines' to find out what is suggested as well as what is actually said. Here are some examples.

Comment 1

You have given an adequate introduction to this topic based on your reading.

The word 'adequate' means 'good enough'. The marker may be saying that what you have written is a pass but not great.

Comment 2

The essay fits in with the word length and keeps to the topic.

If the marker says that the essay is the right length and on the topic but says nothing about the quality of the essay, then it sounds as if there are some problems.

1.   Praise and suggestions

Occasionally students say they don't understand why they got a high mark. Some comments, like the following, are helpful because they tell students exactly what they did well.

You have completed another highly competent essay, starting with a very clear overview of the topic and moving then to the specifics.

However, many essays are not all good or all weak. Markers may tell you some particular thing which you have done well, as in this example, which praises the student's writing and use of references. Notice, though, the phrase 'in most parts of the essay'. It sounds as if there were a few parts where this was not the case.

The introduction and conclusion are well organised. You have a highly readable style and, in most parts of the essay, material is synthesised from a number of sources into a coherent whole.

synthesised	=	put together
a number of sources	=	many different books or articles
a coherent whole	=	a piece of writing that reads well

Here is another comment with praise as well as a suggestion.

Your summary of the various sources is thorough. Ideally you would integrate these more, rather than referring to the various people one by one in each section. You start to do this towards the end of the essay.

2.   Recognising criticisms

Look for criticisms as well as for praise in the comments. Words like 'weakness' and 'problem' are easily recognised as criticism, as in this example where the student has not done enough reading.

One weakness, though, is in the extent of your reading.

Sometimes, though, the criticism is not so clear. Notice the word 'almost' in this next comment.

You write well in a clear, academic style, following the conventions in almost every respect.

academic style   =   university writing
in almost every respect =   most of the time

Some markers say what is good and the student can 'read between the lines' to see the criticism. What do you think is the problem here?

The strength of this essay is in the second part, where you provide your own examples, and in the readability of your style.

Because the marker is praising the second half by saying this is the strong part, that probably means that the first half is not so strong.

The most helpful comments include advice and examples of the problem, as in the following.

You need to master the conventions of university essay writing. Do you realise that you have used direct quotes without acknowledging them? This is a definite NO in any kind of academic writing.

the conventions =   what you are supposed to do
direct quotes   =   someone else's words

Even more helpful is the feedback which tells you what to do about the problem, as in the following three examples.

I recommend a Student Learning Centre workshop.

Keep in touch with other students via the discussions online and any other groups they are forming. This will help you with the concepts as well as with accessing more reading material.

The style will come as you read more and more.

Most markers do not mark every language mistake you make in your essay but rather make a general comment about a problem. For example, in the following comment there is one general criticism, one example, and one suggestion of what to do about it.

Remember to leave time for proofreading. One or two little slips would have been seen if you had had time to read your essay over before handing it in, e.g. the p. 9 list is not in alphabetical order.

Some criticism, like the following, reminds you that you have not followed the essay requirements.

For this essay students were asked to 'review the literature'. Your review is based almost entirely on two sources. Although you list other sources on p. 9 these do not have a mention in the essay.

Comments for the whole class

Another way that markers may give feedback is to give the same comments to everyone. This may be in the form of a checklist or typed comments.

1. Checklists

Some departments have lists of points which essay writers should follow, such as the right length, keeping to the subject, and so on. The marker then ticks these points or gives a grade to show how well a particular point has been followed.

Here is one example of a checklist for markers.

Media assignment

Name . . . .

Here is some individual feedback so that you can see what went well in the essay and what you could improve. The marks for this essay and for the summaries through the course are at the end.

Was there a title?   *Yes / No*

Were there signs of planning? (brainstorm or outline or . . . .)
Yes / No

Did the essay have a clear shape?

compare and contrast / categorise / process / cause and effect / no visible shape

What information was in the introduction?

---

background information / thesis statement / preview of structure

How clear and accurate was the referencing?

distinction between your words and other people's
quotes and paraphrases acknowledged
minimal referencing
details not clear

Were the paragraphs linked clearly?   Yes / Usually / Sometimes / No

What was good about the conclusion?

different from the introduction
strong statement

essay mark   /10   **mark for the 10 summaries**   /5

---

2. Typed comments

In big classes the marker may give out the same page of typed comments for everyone, telling you what was good and not so good about all the essays. In this case you need to see which comments apply to your essay and which are for other people, unless the teacher has marked the parts that are for you.

▶ Peer- and self-evaluation

We have already mentioned that it is a good idea to have another person read your final essay. In some study centres or writing classes students are shown how to do this and they are also given advice on evaluating their own writing.

Peer feedback

Peer feedback means students commenting on other students' writing, either on the final essay or on an earlier draft. Why is peer feedback helpful? One reason is that different readers can see different points that could be improved. Another is that it is sometimes easier to see the strengths and weaknesses of an essay you have not spent hours on yourself. Thirdly, by helping others with their writing, you learn to look at your own more critically. This will help you to develop the skills you need to check your own writing in the future.

Here is some advice on giving peer feedback. It is taken from a sheet given to one group of students in a university self-access centre.

1.   Decide whether you are looking at content or language

First, decide whether you are looking at *what* the other student is saying or *how* he or she says it. The 'what' is the content and the 'how' is the student's language and the way the essay is organised.

Looking at the details of the language is what students usually think of first when they proofread an essay. They check the grammar, the words and the way ideas are joined. However, the organisation of the essay is very important too. For example, you could give feedback on the introduction to the essay by answering these questions.

- Does the introduction clearly state the topic?
- Is there any background or general information about the topic?
- Does the writer state the importance of the topic?
- Does the introduction progress from general to specific?

2.   Start by commenting on the strengths

When you give feedback, the other student wants to know what could be better but also what is good. Some people say that it's more encouraging, and easier to accept criticism, if you mention the good points first. Even if the text is not perfect, it may have taken the author a long time and a lot of effort to write.

To think of what the strengths are, try asking yourself, 'What do I like about this text? What is really good about it?' You could decide that the vocabulary is well chosen, the sentences are clear and varied, or the points are logically presented.

3.   Talk, instead of writing, your feedback

Another way to give feedback is to discuss the essay with the writer as you read it, rather than writing all your comments at the end. Talk with the student writer about the points that you didn't understand, trying to find out what the author meant. Then you could suggest ways to make the writing clearer. As you read each other's work you can ask yourself questions like these:

- Is this really clear?
- If not, what is the problem?
- Would a different word help?
- Would it be better to make two shorter sentences?

Talking about the essay takes more time but it makes the feedback more of a learning experience for both of you.

Evaluating your own work

The final way of finding out about your writing is to 'judge' it yourself. We call this 'self-assessment' or 'self-evaluation'. The best time to do this evaluating is on the final draft of the essay but leave it for a day or two after writing it. Here is one example of a check sheet.

Check your assignment yourself

The topic

- Does your title match the title given?   *yes / no / partly*
- Does the essay keep to the topic?   all the time / mostly

The expression and shape

- Can you read your essay aloud and understand it?   *yes / no*
- Does your essay follow a clear pattern?   *yes / no*

The introduction

- Is there an thesis statement?   yes / no
- Have you announced the essay pattern?   yes / no

The body

- Which pattern did you follow?   parallel? linear?
- How many different points did you make?   . . . .
- Are they supported with examples?   yes / no
- Is there a mixture of quotes and paraphrases?   yes / no

The conclusion

- Did you summarise the points briefly?   yes / no
- Did you vary the words slightly from the introduction?   yes / no
- Did you have a strong final statement?   yes / no

Making use of feedback

When you are given feedback by the teacher or by another student, take time to think about it. Here are some notes that were written for one group of students to show how they could use feedback from other students.

Try to see why your fellow student made particular comments. If you don't understand why your friend commented on a certain point, then ask him or her what was unclear and why.

Don't forget: you don't have to agree with everything others say. You may disagree with them, because their feedback is just an opinion. However, if they misunderstood what you wrote, this could mean that the marker may misunderstand it too. You need to rewrite your text.

Don't be put off if they have negative comments. You can learn from these as well!

In this chapter we have talked about ways of being a better writer. Writing is not separate from other skills. The more you read, the more you will find out about words and how to put them together. The more you listen, the more ideas you will collect, and of course the more you speak, the clearer your ideas will become.

Writing at university is a huge subject. You can read more about it in these books in this same Palgrave Study Guides series:

How to Write Better Essays, by Bryan Greetham (2001), takes you through the stages of essay writing from understanding the question to research, planning, writing and revision.

The Mature Student's Guide to Writing, by Jean Rose (2001), has one chapter on getting your language right, one on essay writing and the rest on other types of writing: poetry and reports for example.

Many handbooks for students are addressed to particular disciplines. For example, the following is addressed to science/engineering students:

Silyn-Roberts, Heather (1996) *Writing for Science* (Auckland: Addison Wesley Longman).

Answer to 'test yourself' (p. 136)

Finally, here is one suggested way of grouping the student's ideas for an essay.

Language learners can help themselves

Introduction
    Reasons for self-help
    Range of informal and formal opportunities
    Comparison of formal and informal learning
    Announcement of essay plan

Formal learning opportunities
    Choosing the right course
    Finding the right level of class
    Making the most of class time
    Using textbooks out of class

Informal learning opportunities
    Examples of informal opportunities
    Ways of learning informally
        Listening to the radio
        Finding opportunities to talk

Problems and overcoming them
    Shortage of time
        Time management
    Shyness

Conclusion
    Summary of learners' roles
    Encouragement to get started

8 Writing a Thesis

In Chapter 2 you read about planning your postgraduate programme. One important part of this programme may be the writing of a thesis or dissertation. In this chapter you will find suggestions for making this writing process interesting and enjoyable.

This chapter answers the following questions:

- In what order do students undertake the writing of a thesis?
- What does a supervisor do?
- How can students and supervisors work together?

▶ Steps in writing a thesis

Summary of the steps
Here is a simplified list of the work you do for a thesis. After each stage there is a list of questions you need to answer. The answers differ from one department to another. We go on to discuss the steps in more detail.

1. Decide on a topic.
   - What subject interests you?
   - Talk with a lecturer about possible topics.
   - How will you find information on this topic?

2. Start (and continue!) reading.
   - What reading lists do you already have on this topic?
   - Where else could you get reading lists?

3. Write a proposal.
   - What does a proposal look like in your department?
   - Are there any guidelines or examples available?

4. Find and meet regularly with a supervisor.
    *   How does this department arrange supervision?
    *   Are students allowed to ask for a particular supervisor?
    *   How often does the supervisor want to see you?
    *   How can you contact him/her (see Chapter 9)?

5. Collect and analyse your data.
    *   Where and how will you collect data?
    *   Which type of analysis suits the data best?

6. Write up the results.
    *   Are there any examples of theses in the library?
    *   Is there a seminar on writing up results?
    *   Who can help you with the proofreading?

7. Hand in your thesis.
    *   Where exactly do you hand in your thesis?
    *   How is it supposed to be bound?
    *   How many copies do you need?

8. Maybe write an article.
    *   Can you write an article together with your supervisor?

This list of questions makes the process seem very easy and step by step. In fact, you are doing many of these things at the same time. Here are more details about some of these steps. We do not go into detail on every step, such as analysing data, because so many good books have been written on research methods.

Choosing a topic

Choosing a research topic is a very big step. Because you will be working on the topic for a long time it should be something that interests you and it also needs to be original (new) in some way. One way to decide is to read about some possible topics and listen to suggestions from senior people in the department. Here are some questions that you and your supervisor could discuss.

*   Which topics have interested you in your course so far?
    *   Why could they be worth studying further?
    *   What have other people already said on these topics?
    *   How could your study add to theirs?

- Is your supervisor working on a project you could join? (See more below on joint research projects.)
- In your study area what questions are researchers asking?

Once you have a topic (or general area of interest) you must decide on an exact question or questions, or a hypothesis that you want to test. A hypothesis is something people think may be true but that they are not yet sure about. Your study will test this hypothesis (find out if it is true). Consider what problems there could be in answering this question or testing this hypothesis. Is it small enough? Big enough?

If you decide to change the topic and you have started reading, then you should discuss this as soon as possible with your supervisor. The supervisor may have been chosen because he or she has a special interest in your topic and if you change your topic completely then it may be that you need a different supervisor.

Your reading

Chapter 6 has suggestions about your reading.

Writing a proposal

Once you have chosen a topic you write a proposal, which will be read by people in the department where you hope to study. In fact if you are starting at a new university as a postgraduate student you may have to write a proposal before being accepted for the programme and getting the official letter which allows you to make the visa arrangements.

As well as being necessary for enrolment, there are several other reasons for writing a proposal. One is that putting your ideas into words helps you to think clearly. Another reason is that the proposal lets the supervisor give you help by giving answers to these and other questions.

Can these research questions be answered?
Does the timetable look possible?
What possible problems could there be?

Another reason for writing a proposal is to make you take the first step towards the research. Once your proposal is written, you have some kind of timetable for planning each month's work. Your proposal is like the framework for the final thesis.

Occasionally, too, proposals are needed to get money for your research. Perhaps your supervisor has money available for a big project and your work will be a small part of it.

Here, one student talks about how he started to write a proposal:

I thought about my PhD for a long time. I had written an MA thesis before and knew I really wanted to do something that I found very interesting, not just something my supervisor would like. I read a lot of books and articles on topics that appealed to me and this way realised more and more what I wanted to do, what I really wanted to find out for myself. I wanted to apply for a scholarship and had two months before the deadline. I emailed my supervisor with a proposal and he gave me feedback. There were many things that I hadn't thought of enough. It helped me to start reading more specifically to find the answers to the questions I was interested in. I sent a new proposal to my supervisor and got it back, revised it and sent it back, and this continued for a few more times until it was more clear what I was going to investigate. Instead of looking at five different things, I was now only going to look at two things . . .

A good proposal tries to answer some important questions about your research:

1. **Where and how will you look for answers?**
   What, and how many, people and places will be involved?

2. **Why did you choose this research method?**
   For your research there are many ways of collecting information. You may design a questionnaire, collect a case study, do interviews. Your methods need to suit your questions and in your proposal you need to say why you chose a certain method.

3. **What data will you be collecting?**
   From whom? How much data? How do you plan to interpret the data?

4. **The research plan (timetable)**
   • What will you be doing, and when, through the year?
   • What are the actual steps in the research?
   • By what date do you aim to complete each step?

5. **Do you expect any problems?**
   What have been the difficulties with similar research?

When your proposal has been accepted by your supervisor and the department's Postgraduate Committee, and the university has accepted your enrolment, you are ready to start your research.

Writing up the thesis

When you have finished doing your research it is time to write up the final results. A thesis is written in a certain 'genre' or style of writing. If you are not sure what this style is, try reading one or two theses in the library or attend a workshop at the Student Learning Centre to find out more.

Of course you will have been writing parts all the way. For example, as you plan the methods, you write up the relevant chapter, and so on. Have a look at Table 23, which shows you all the different parts of a thesis and what should go in them. The left-hand column is also very similar to your final Table of Contents.

Table 23 Parts of a thesis

The section	What does it do?
Abstract	1. Gives some background information. 2. Says what you did and what you found. 3. Reports your conclusion.
Introduction	1. Says what is new about your work. 2. Says why you chose this topic.
Methods	Describes the way you tried to find the answers to your research questions.
Results	Gives the answers (if you found them!) to the research questions.
Discussion	1. Shows what the results mean and says which questions could and could not be answered. 2. Discusses any new questions that the research brings up.
Conclusion	1. Briefly lists the main findings of the research. 2. Describes what the results mean for other people. (Shows how the results help people who work in that field.)

When students start writing their final thesis there are some details which are important.

1. Referencing

Referencing is the way you mention the sources you have been reading. As we saw in Chapter 7, markers are strict about work which does not follow the format for acknowledging other people's work.

2. Voice

'Voice' is another word for the 'tone' of the writing. It is quite common for students to sound too certain by saying something like this:

A definitely caused **B** to happen . . .

This sentence makes it sound as if there is absolutely no doubt about the point. Most of the time this is not the case. In university writing, therefore, people use phrases like 'it seems likely that', or 'it appears that' in conclusions. Look at this example:

> In these experiments **A** appeared to cause **B** to happen. It is possible then, that this would happen in other circumstances as well because . . .

Here the author explains that in one situation (i.e. during the experiments in the research) **A** and **B** appeared to be linked. There could have been other causes as well.

Here are some phrases you could use to make sure your writing is not too definite:

> It is likely that . . .

> It is possible that . . .

> It could be that . . .

> The results seem to show that . . .

On the other hand, in some subjects if your results strongly support a certain conclusion then you can use expressions such as:

> This shows that . . .

> It is clear that . . .

> From this we see that . . .

> It can be concluded that . . .

Proofreading

At the final stage before handing in your thesis you need to make sure that there are no grammatical mistakes or typing errors. Your supervisor is not the person to do this. A good proofreader does not have to know anything about your subject but does need to be good at English and know about university writing. Sometimes students are pleased to proofread the work of students one or two years ahead of them because it gives them an idea of what to expect for themselves. If you know someone who is planning to do a dissertation next year, try asking them, because it might help them later when they come to do their own. You will need to discuss first whether the person is willing to do it for the experience, or out of kindness, or for money. Another idea is to ask if retired university staff are available to proofread students' work. Ask your supervisor who (s)he can recommend. Some common problems to look for in proofreading are listed in Table 24.

Table 24   Proofreading problems

Common problems	Suggestions
Punctuation, spelling and grammar	• Use the Spellcheck. • Ask someone else to proofread for you.
Paragraphs in the wrong places	• Leave at least a week between writing and changing the order.
The same words all the time.	• Identify the repeats through the 'Find' function. • Use a thesaurus to find synonyms.
The wrong words.	• Ask a native speaker to check and make suggestions.

Handing in your thesis

You are expected to hand in a bound book, which will probably be kept in the library of your university or department. One other stage can follow handing in the thesis. You (alone or with your supervisor) may publish an article as a result of what you have found in your study (see below).

Final word

Here is one last word about writing a thesis and doing a PhD. It can be a lonely life, particularly if you have just changed countries and don't know anybody, but it doesn't have to be that way.

In most departments there are places where you can meet other PhD students. This may be a room with comfortable chairs and a coffee machine or it may be a place with computers and study tables. As well as a place to meet, there may be special times for students to talk together about their work (seminars or discussion groups). They will all be studying different topics but they can learn from the way others are studying. Many students say they get a lot of help from other students, even those doing quite different subjects. One group of overseas students said why they liked meeting with others once a fortnight:

It encouraged me. I was not the only one to sometimes feel stupid and slow.

I could ask the students questions I couldn't ask the supervisor because I was afraid I should know the answer.

Each time someone would tell us some new hint like how to use a different type of computer search.

If you would like to read more on this topic, many books have been written to help you. One is a guide in the Palgrave Study Skills Series by Gina Wisker called *The Postgraduate Research Handbook*. Another very useful book in the same series is *Authoring a PhD* by Patrick Dunleavy. You will probably also find titles covering research about your particular subject.

▶ Working with a supervisor

Your supervisor is the person who works with you one-to-one as you do the research, and who may also help you decide on a topic. He or she may be the professor or lecturer. As we noted earlier, there are plenty of books that tell you how to do the research but in this section we are talking just about working with your supervisor.

How does supervision 'work'?

Students (and some lecturers) are not always sure about the 'rules' of supervision. Even if your department has written guidelines, people in the same department may have a different understanding of what they mean. Here are a few questions that students sometimes ask.

Do I choose my own supervisor?
What if I don't like the supervisor they offer me?
How often do students and supervisors meet?
Will the supervisor help me with all my problems?

In the following example you will see that there is more than one answer to the question of how supervision works. Two students near the beginning of their MA theses are talking about their supervisors.

Student 1:   I see my supervisor once a fortnight. How about you?
Student 2:   My supervisor doesn't tell me how often to come. I don't want to annoy her by going too often. She's very busy.
Student 1:   But what does she say at the end of a session?

| Student 2: | She usually says something vague like 'I'll look forward to seeing those questions when you've had another look at them.' What does that mean? Will she contact me? |
| Student 1: | Probably it means you are the one who should make the contact. |

Usually at the end of a meeting you and your supervisor will decide when to see each other again, or what you need to do before there is anything to talk about. Perhaps you need to read more, or design an experiment, or write a questionnaire, or rewrite one section of your work. Rewriting sections is a normal part of the process. At the next meeting your supervisor will ask to see what you have done or may ask you about the literature you have read. Ask if you should send the pages beforehand so that the supervisor has time to read and think about your work.

What happens at each meeting depends partly on your supervisor and partly on you. The meetings are a time to discuss problems, to report the progress you have made, to talk about what you can do next. Your supervisor may ask you questions and of course you will have questions too. For example, the session may start with a question:

Did you have any problems?

How have things been going?

Were you able to . . . ?

You, too, can ask questions. If you cannot find all the books and articles you need, then you could mention this to the supervisor. It takes some time to get used to a new library system. For example, the supervisor may tell you that there is a special librarian for your subject who can help you find the books you want. If you have found the books and articles you want but can't understand some point in them, then you could mention that too.

When it comes to planning how to collect your data collection, you might have more to ask the supervisor. For example, if you have problems in developing the questionnaire, tell your supervisor and ask for help. If you don't mention your difficulty he or she will think that there were no problems. It is a good idea to write down all the questions you come up with between sessions so that you don't forget them the next time you meet.

How often do we meet?
The question of how often supervisors and students should meet is, perhaps, the first thing to decide. As we see from the comments of two more students, people might have different ideas.

Student 3

He always expects me to do a lot before we meet but sometimes I'd rather put off our meeting till I've done something.

Student 3 has a good point. If for some reason you were not able to do what you agreed on with your supervisor, say so before the session. It may be a better idea to reschedule the appointment until you have done your work. It is very important to say why you are putting off your meeting. Rather than just leaving a message on the answerphone to say 'I'm sorry I can't come tomorrow', say 'I'm sorry I haven't finished all that reading you gave me. Would you like me to come anyway or should we make another appointment.' Then the supervisor understands your problem and may suggest meeting anyway for a talk.

Student 4

Sometimes I think my supervisor wants me to go away for a long time before our next meeting but I'm not sure.

The problem here is that the supervisor may not mean this. The idea of going away for a long time may or may not be what was meant. It is true that some people do rely on their supervisor too much, especially if they are from countries where university teachers look after their students more closely, and in that case a supervisor may try to encourage the person to be more independent.

Although in Western universities students are expected to be independent, this does not mean spending weeks and weeks without any contact. If you do this you may find you have gone away on some wrong track and therefore a lot of your work turns out to have been for nothing. It is a student's responsibility to keep in regular contact with the supervisor but it can be difficult to find the right balance. Ask other students and ask the supervisor.

Who does what?

As well as finding out how often to meet, students need to know how much help they can expect from their supervisor. Students who are writing a thesis or dissertation are sometimes not sure how much help to expect. Universities run workshops to tell students what to expect and other workshops to tell supervisors how to work with their students. Here are examples of what one supervisor and one student said about their roles. As these comments show, it's important to talk openly about what is happening.

A supervisor

I'm not sure if X really understands that it's not my job to proofread every chapter.

A student

My supervisor seems to expect me to do a lot of work myself on the draft copies, even though I keep giving her the chapters in good time before we meet.

The answer to this sort of misunderstanding is to talk about the arrangements, just as you would with a friend if you were having trouble understanding some arrangements. Don't be afraid to say:

I wasn't sure last time if you meant . . .

Do you mean that I should . . . ?

We asked several supervisors and students the questions, 'What has to be done for a thesis?' and 'Who does it?' Table 25 shows what most people said about the steps in writing a thesis and how they are divided up. 'Both' means the student and supervisor together.

Table 25   Supervisor and student roles

Task	Who does it?
1 Choosing a topic	Both
2 Reading about the topic	Student
3 Planning the research method	Both
4 Changing the topic	Both
5 Collecting the data	Student
6 Analysing the data	Mainly the student
7 Writing up the results	Student
8 Proofreading	Other people

You will notice one or two things from this table. First, there is no part of the process where the supervisor works alone, although of course he or she gives comments all the time on drafts. Some stages, such as collecting the data, are definitely the work of the student. Of course the supervisor will give ideas about where and how to collect data but the student actually does it. When it comes to analysing the data there will be discussions between both parties but the student should arrive at the meeting with some ideas. Instead of asking the supervisor: 'What does this show?', it is better to show that you have been thinking, by saying something like this:

It looks as if . . .

I think . . . What do you think?

Writing up the results is definitely your work. The supervisor will read it from time to time but the actual writing is your work.

What is a 'second' supervisor?

Sometimes students have a second supervisor, also called a co-supervisor or joint supervisor. Perhaps the subject you have chosen covers two different areas or perhaps the main supervisor is very busy and would not be free to see you often enough. If the main supervisor does not know everything about your topic, the second supervisor can fill in the gaps. Some people, like this student, have other reasons for having a second supervisor:

My supervisor is very good in the field I'm doing research in and his comments are very useful. But he is not very motivating or helpful when things are not going well for me and I feel discouraged. With my second supervisor I have more contact and it's more personal. Together they are an excellent team!

What should I do if I am not happy with my supervisor?

This is a difficult question. If you know before you start your study that it will be difficult for you to work with the supervisor you have been given, talk to someone in the department. Maybe you can have a different staff member. If things are difficult after you have started work, then again you need to talk to someone. If you cannot talk to the supervisor about the problem then find the person in the department who organises your study, perhaps the graduate supervisor. If you study in a small department or, for some other reason, don't feel comfortable talking to someone who is one of your supervisor's colleagues, you can often get help and advice from your faculty's postgraduate office.

Writing joint articles

When all your work is over your lecturer might say, 'Would you like to try to get this published?' If you agree, then your work can become an article to be read by more people. If you write a joint article with your supervisor then both your names are printed in the journal. The advantage of a joint article is that the supervisor probably knows how to write articles in the right style for journals. If you write the article by yourself with just a few suggestions from the lecturer, the advantage is that you have an article in your name alone.

Part III
University Life

Introduction

So far in this book we have talked about getting to university and then making the most of your study time there. The final section of this book goes beyond your university study to discuss the importance of communicating with your fellow students and your teachers or lecturers. There is also a chapter on dealing with problems that may arise. All students can experience problems in a new situation, but these can seem worse for students who are living far from their home country. Support is available for you.

The book ends with ideas for enjoying life at university apart from your studies. Whatever subject you are studying, something in this section will apply to you.

9 Communicating with Staff and Students

Who are all the people and places you can visit during your studies? This chapter starts by naming some of the offices and people who are there to support you in organising your studies. Why do staff and students have discussions? We hear answers to this question from some of the people involved. Once you know where to find people and why you would like to talk with them, the next question is how to make contact. Then there is information about how to be in touch with staff in their offices, by email or telephone and through the course website. We also talk about the different ways you can communicate with other students on the course.

This chapter answers the following questions:

- Which places and people should students be contacting?
- When do students contact staff?
- What are the best ways to make contact?
- How do students contact one another out of class?

▶ Places and people

Once you start university you will hear people talking like this:

In this department . . .

The departmental office is the place to go for . . .

X is in another department.

The Arts Faculty has 6000 students.

You need to get the dean's signature.

You will come to know some of the places around the university as you visit them for your enrolment and you will gradually recognise people by name or by face, but at first it's helpful to know in general what to expect. Here is some information about places and people at university, although the actual names may be different from one university to another.

The parts of the university

The big divisions of the university are the *campus* (the place where your part of the university is), the *faculty* (a group of departments teaching similar subjects) and the *department* (the part of the university that teaches your subject). Let's see in detail what each of these means.

1. The campus

The campus is the place where all the university buildings are. Your university may have more than one campus in the same city and even in more than one city or country.

If you are applying to study at university Z in City X, you may find that the Science Faculty is at a campus in one part of town and the Commerce Faculty in another campus elsewhere. When you are enrolling you will find out this information. There will probably be a student cafeteria, cash machines, a library and computer facilities on all the campuses. Also, if there is more than one campus in a city there is probably free transportation for students between the different campuses.

2. The faculty

The word 'faculty' has different meanings in America and Britain, and in the countries that follow the tradition of each of these countries. In the United States the word 'faculty' means the teaching staff at a university. In the British system the university is divided into a number of faculties. (These are called 'colleges' or 'schools' in the United States.) We use the British meaning in this book.

Students belong to one faculty, or occasionally two. If you are studying for a BA, and taking subjects like languages, literature, history and so on, then you are in the Arts Faculty. Other students will be studying in the Faculty of Science, Faculty of Engineering, Faculty of Business and Economics, Faculty of Law etc. A few subjects, such as psychology, geography or computer studies, could be part of more than one degree and faculty.

Often faculties have their own information centres. These could be called:

the Faculty Office;
the Faculty Student Centre;

the Undergraduate Centre;
the Postgraduate Centre.

At these places you can get specific advice about your courses, including help with planning your degree and information about scholarships. Many faculties also have a (small) library to make it easy for their students to get books about the subjects taught there, especially if the university library is far away.

The faculty may also have other services such as a careers advisory centre where graduates and students can get help with finding a job. Some faculties even have their own student organisations, which help students and organise social events. These can be a good way to get to know new people with similar interests.

Another big division is a School, as in 'the School of Asian Languages'. This may be like a faculty or a department, only bigger.

3. The department
The next size down is the department. You will hear students say, 'I study in the History Department.' A department may have two or more smaller sections to it, each for a different part of History studies. When people study for a major, most of their courses are probably taught in one department, with other minor courses in other departments.

Your lecturers all belong to a particular department where they have their offices, their staff room and their meetings. Departments, like faculties, sometimes provide an extra study room specially for students, or a welcome at the start of the semester.

The people
In all these campuses, faculties and departments there are staff: teachers and administrators. Your university calendar will have lists of these people's names and titles.

1. The university leaders
There are some university staff whom you will probably not meet personally, although you will see them at the graduation ceremony and other formal occasions. The university leader is usually called a vice-chancellor (VC). This person is helped by a 'deputy vice-chancellor' or 'assistant vice-chancellor'. At technical universities and at some recently established universities the term CEO (chief executive officer) is sometimes used instead of vice-chancellor. American universities often have a president.

The head of a faculty is called a dean. Deans are usually appointed for a fixed period of time such as two years or five years, after which they return to their departments and continue teaching. Sometimes at enrolment you need the 'dean's signature', although other staff are usually in the office to sign for the dean.

2. The department staff

The next group of people are those who will actually be teaching you. They are in your department and have one of the following titles:

Professor
Associate professor
Senior lecturer
Lecturer
Senior tutor
Tutor or instructor
Teaching assistant (TA)

These titles tell you about how senior the people are, with the professor being the most senior and the tutors or teaching assistants (TAs) the most junior. ('Senior' means the position at the university, not the person's actual age.) Your courses may be taught by any of these people, although TAs are often graduate students who assist lecturers or who teach lower-level courses.

In some countries, like the United States, a professor means anyone who teaches at a university, but in countries that follow the British system a professor is a senior person with a doctorate (PhD) who has worked in a certain field for many years and has built up a good academic reputation.

As well as the titles that tell you about how senior they are, the same people have other titles which tell you about their non-teaching work. One person (usually a professor or associate professor) is also the Head of Department (HoD), who organises the work of the department. You may need to have this person's signature if you are asking for permission to enrol for a course where you don't have the prerequisites (Chapter 1 explained about exemptions).

Other people have special tasks. Here are some of them:

• *The graduate advisor* is the person to visit if you are planning to study for a higher degree.

• *The undergraduate advisor* helps you plan your courses so that you have the best possible mixture of subjects.

Non-teaching staff

While enrolling you will have had some contact with staff, particularly the international student officers (see below). The next people you meet at your new university will probably be the administrative staff. These have various titles (secretary, office manager, administrative assistant) and their job is to help you enrol at the start of your course and find your way around for the rest of the year. They work in various parts of the university and, of course, the names of their offices vary from place to place, but in Table 26 there are some places and people to look out for.

Some details of other staff are now given.

• *Disability officers* work with people who need special help with their studies for short-term or long-term reasons. Here is one example of how a disability officer was able to help a student.

Student X moved around in a wheelchair. She found that while most of her lecture rooms could be reached, one had difficult access for wheelchairs. She talked to the disability officer, who arranged for two classes to exchange lecture rooms. The problem was solved.

• *University counsellors* work with students who have personal problems of any type. If you have difficulty concentrating or if you feel unhappy, then university counsellors are the people to see. Perhaps you are working under too much stress because your schedule is too full, or maybe you feel lonely because you find it difficult to make friends in a new country. You could have other, personal problems that you would like to talk about.

No problem is too big or too small for counsellors. They are there for you, will listen to you and will try to help you or direct you to people who can. Find out where their offices are and call in. You may be asked to make an appointment but if the problem is urgent they will usually see you immediately. See the next chapter for more on coping with problems.

International offices

Most universities in English-speaking countries have an International Office for students from other countries. You can contact the international offices by letter, phone or email as soon as you start thinking about studying at their university. They can do the following things for you:

• answer your questions about the university's admission requirements;
• tell you about fees and any available scholarships or sponsorships;
• help you fill in your application documents;

Table 26 University services

Where?	What?
The university registry	Answers general questions. Gives information about fees.
Accommodation service	Gives general information about public accommodation. Organises accommodation in the university Halls of Residence.
Student services (Students' association)	Offers general support. Provides sports areas. May have emergency money for students. Lists part-time jobs.
Faculty office	Gives handbooks about degrees. Directs students to the right department.
Department office	Answers questions about courses. Tells you where to find teaching staff. Gives information about enrolment.
Student loans and allowances	Organises and pays out money to those who are eligible.
Chaplaincy	Provides spiritual support for students. Organises events to support students generally. May provide a place for students to hold religious services.
Childcare services	Provides daycare for the pre-school children of students and staff.
Careers and Employment Office	Gives information about various careers. Provides names of people available for individual discussions about future jobs.
University bookshop	Sells textbooks, calendars, stationery.
Student Learning Centre	Organises extra classes (see Chapter 10).

- give advice on preparing for your departure;
- possibly arrange travel and pick you up from the airport.

Some universities and international offices also have staff who work overseas. These people can advise you, often in your own language, on anything about your study plans. To give you an idea, Nottingham, an average sized university in the United Kingdom, has 48 representatives all around the world, of which six are in China alone! You have a good chance of finding an office near you. The best way to check is on the university website. Click on 'students' or 'prospective students' (prospective means they are not enrolled yet) and generally you will find a link to the International (Students') Office's homepage where you can find a list of overseas representatives.

After you arrive, the International Office can also give help with accommodation, or English support, or advice about where to go for more help. Often you and your family can contact the International Office in an emergency. They can help you to find a lawyer or a doctor who speaks your language and they can contact your family overseas. Finally, almost all the International Offices organise an 'orientation' for international students. The orientation is an excellent way of getting to know your university, meeting new people and learning about the country. Figure 9 shows an example of one university's orientation programme.

Another place to look for information about studying at your new university is in the International Students' Information Guide, which is prepared by many universities to help students find accommodation, learn about the city, read about the national cultures and many other things which are important to life in a new country. There is also a general Student Handbook, which

f Auckland | Te Waananga O Waipapa   Text Version

VISITORS | STUDENTS | STAFF | COMMUNITY | FACULTIES & DEPARTMENTS | RESEARCH | NEWS | RESOURCES | CONTACTS

International Students Orientation Programme

In an effort to make your stay rewarding and memorable, and to help you achieve your academic goals, the International Office provides an orientation programme for all new international students. The three day programme, which is held during the week before classes begin, offers new students a range of services and opportunities, and is designed to:

- make you feel welcome, and get you settled in before your classes begin,
- present you with general information about living and studying at the University of Auckland,
- provide information on the range of services and facilities available to our students on campus,
- offer some advice on strategies for getting the most out of your studies so that you will succeed academically (this is done in conjunction with the Student Learning Centre),
- introduce you to the unique culture, as well as the beautiful landscap around Auckland City,
- and best of all, the Orientation Programme offers plenty of opportunity to meet other international students like yourself!

The International Students Orientation Programme is FREE to all new international students.

Figure 9   University orientation programme

is a guide published every year for all students (not only those from other countries). This contains information about almost every part of university life and can often be ordered from overseas.

▶ Reasons for contacting staff

As the examples in this section show, students may contact university staff about any topic related to studies. We asked staff to tell us the most common reasons why students came to their offices or emailed them. Here is their list.

Advice on course planning

Before each semester starts, the most common reasons for students being in touch is to talk about which courses to take. We saw in the previous chapter that there is usually one staff member who has the job of giving course advice if you already know your subject. You should ask at the Department Office for the name of that person, or ask at the Faculty Office if you know only that you want to do a particular type of degree. Thus if you wanted to study for a BA you would go to the Faculty of Arts office.

For many courses now you can enrol online without talking to any staff. This is fine if you are sure that you know what subjects you want to study, but the computer programme may stop you from enrolling for subjects that do not fit your degree. Sometimes a staff member can give you an exemption so that you can study a combination of subjects that suits you better than the subjects listed.

Changing a tutorial time

Once the course has started, there are other reasons for being in touch with staff, such as changing the time of a tutorial. At the start of a course, your name will be on a list of tutorial times. (If they allow you to sign up for your favourite time, be early. Certains times of the day fill up fast.) If the time you are given is not suitable, see a staff member or check at the office. To save time, ask first for the name of the person who makes these changes. Then give a clear reason. For example:

> I'm sorry, I can't take the afternoon tutorial because I work from two o'clock.

Leaving a course

A third reason for contacting staff happens usually just before or just after the classes start. Students find that the subjects they have chosen are not the right ones for some reason. If you are already enrolled in a course, then it is important to discuss this problem with someone. If you simply stop coming to class, then the university records may show 'FAIL' at the end. It is better to go and tell someone that you are leaving the course so that your records show that you have withdrawn formally.

Sometimes it is not necessary to leave the course. For example, if you are late with an assignment because of illness and you have a doctor's certificate, you can sometimes make up late work if you tell the lecturer why you are thinking of stopping. There may be other problems which allow you to be late but these need to be discussed.

Questions about lectures

Students sometimes ask to see staff in their offices with questions about a lecture, especially if there was no question time and no tutorials. Again, make it clear why you have come. For example, you can say:

Last week in the lecture you talked about X. I have read the chapter in the course book, but I still don't understand what X means.

In Chapter 4 we discussed ways of asking questions in lectures.

Asking about assignments

One of the most common reasons for contacting staff is questions about assignments. Students ask questions before they write an assignment, they ask if they can hand an assignment in late, and thirdly, after an assignment is marked, they go to ask questions again. Let's look at these three reasons in turn.

1.   What is this assignment about?

Before going to a lecturer's office to discuss an assignment, here are some things to check.

*   Has the lecturer promised to discuss the topic in class next week?
    If so, wait for that discussion.
*   Does anyone else want help with the same assignment?
    If two students go to the office together then you can discuss the answers together later.
*   Which lecturer or tutor is the right person to ask?
    Ask other students or someone in the office.

2.   May I hand this assignment in late?

Having extra time for an assignment is called 'getting an extension'. As you can imagine, asking for permission to hand in an assignment late is not very popular with lecturers. They may be waiting to hand back the marked assignment with a feedback sheet and of course they can't take in a late assignment after they have done this.

The rules here vary, but generally staff are happier about extensions if there is a really good reason. Check in the departmental handbook. As we saw earlier, if you are ill you can often get an extension by showing a doctor's statement. Mention this clearly when you come to see the lecturer, saying something like:

> *Can I talk to you please? My assignment isn't finished but I have a doctor's certificate to show that I have been ill for one week.*

If the whole class has a problem with the date then it's better for the class representative to go and ask the lecturer for an extension.

3. Questions about marked assignments
As we saw in Chapter 7, when your assignment is returned it will have a mark or grade and also some individual or group comments. If you read all these comments and you still do not understand why you had that grade, then of course you will want to ask about it. When the lecturer has explained, don't leave before you are sure you understand. You could try checking like this:

> *Are you saying that I didn't. . . . ?*
>
> *Was my main problem . . . ?*
>
> *So, would I get a better mark next time if I . . . ?*

Asking for personal references
When senior students need a reference to apply for a scholarship or a job they may ask a staff member who knows them well. However, undergraduate students do not usually ask staff for references.

▶ Office, telephone and email contacts

When you want to arrange a meeting with a staff member, rather than just visiting the office and hoping to find the person free, try more reliable ways. Here are some suggestions.

What's a good time to go to a staff member's office?
The department handbook may answer this question for you, or staff members may have 'Office Hours' notices on their doors. We asked several

university staff the question 'What's a good time for students to go to your office?' and we had four different answers.

I have my office hours printed on the door so students know when to find me in.

They can just drop in any time.

If my door is open students are always welcome. If the door is closed that means I'm busy.

I try to encourage them to make an appointment. Email is a good way.

How do I address my lecturer?
One problem mentioned by some students is what to call their lecturers. The best thing is to ask 'What should I call you?' Some prefer students to call them by their given names (Sandra, Stephen) but some prefer you to address them more formally (Mr Smith, Mrs Andrews, Dr Jones, Professor Rogers). Sometimes there is confusion about this. One student said:

When I first met my supervisor I asked him 'Shall I call you Professor . . .' and he said 'That's fine'. I later found out that everyone else called him by his first name and that he thought, probably because I come from another country with a different culture, that it would be easier for me to address him in a formal way. I'd like to do the same thing as everyone else but now it would be very difficult to change the way I speak to him.

Explain yourself clearly
When you arrive in the office the staff member will greet you and usually ask you to sit down. One problem that staff members report is not knowing why the student has come to see them. Look at this real student–teacher interview in the teacher's office.

Teacher: What can I do for you today?
Student: Ah I've come about my assignment.
Teacher: Assignment. Oh yes. Yep. You've been to the tutorial?
Student: Yes.
Teacher: Yep < 9 seconds > Well, what is the problem with you . . . ?
Student: Ah < 9 seconds > I don't know how to write an issue about a university.
Teacher   Oh OK. etc.[1]

Notice that it took three turns for the student to state the problem. The first pause is for nine seconds, which is not a long time when talking with friends, but it can seem quite long when two people are staring at each other across a desk and other students are waiting outside the door.

Think about the difference between meeting a friend and having a conversation in a shop. With your friend you probably have some 'small talk' first ('How are things? What have you been doing?'). In a shop, on the other hand, you would be wasting the assistant's time if you asked about their health or their weekend when people are standing behind you in a queue. University office conversation is more like talking in a shop. You want something and the lecturer needs to know what it is. Try to come straight to the point.

Will lecturers listen to personal problems?

Universities have counsellors who are trained to listen and give advice on personal problems. Of course (as we saw earlier in the chapter) if you need to hand in an essay late because of personal problems then you will need to explain this to your lecturer but otherwise discussing personal problems is not their real role.

Who decides when the visit is over?

When students have said all they want to say they may wonder, 'Is this discussion over now? Is it OK for me to go?' Try ending with some simple phrase like 'Thank you' and then see if the lecturer asks, 'Is there anything else?' Then you can add another question or say something like 'No thank you, that's all.'

Telephoning staff

Telephoning used to be the most common way for students to contact staff. A student would phone and if the discussion needed more time, the staff member would suggest a time to come in and talk some more. Now that emails are more common, telephone calls are less popular. In fact they can be disturbing if a staff member is busy doing other work or if someone else who has made an appointment is in the office. Before you ring, make sure there is no other way of contacting your teacher, such as coming to the office during visiting hours or sending an email.

If you do telephone, be brief. Ask if this is a good time to talk and then be clear about the purpose of your call. If the person is not there when you telephone, you can leave a message on the voice mail including your name (maybe spell it), your phone number and, if you are in a large class, your ID number. You may not have an immediate reply because the lecturer may wait until there is time to have a good talk with you, or because your details were not clear. Lecturers report difficulties with returning calls because students speak too fast or not clearly enough. Of course there is no point in telephoning from your home country and asking for a return call.

May I phone my lecturer at home?

It is not normal to telephone staff at home. Sometimes a lecturer may give a home phone number to senior students but usually you contact them at work.

Emailing staff

Emailing can be a quick and convenient way to communicate with staff and students. People can send and read emails whenever it suits them. No wonder it is now used more and more by teachers and students. This is what university staff had to say about email:

> *Email has opened up new ways for staff and students to communicate. On the whole it suits me fine. They use it mainly to make appointments with me and I use it mainly to communicate with the class reps.*   [reps = elected representatives]

Another lecturer believed that email was a help in getting to know students better:

> *Every now and then I notice a huge difference between a student's email correspondence and their class image. For example, one student who hardly spoke in class sent a number of lengthy emails. Maybe the impersonal aspect makes it easier for people to 'speak'.*
>
> *Some students want to send their late assignments via email to save time but I'm afraid I've told them it's not my responsibility to print out their work and staple them together.*
>
> *One possible trap with email is that it doesn't make the writer's tone clear. I worry about that sometimes with students whose first language is not English. I might mean to make a helpful suggestion but they take it as a criticism.*

Students, too, have their views about emailing staff. Here are a couple of their comments.

> *I emailed a rough copy of my assignment to my lecturer for her to comment on it but she suggested I should make an appointment to come and discuss it. Why?*

Lecturers don't usually go through the first copy of an essay in detail. Perhaps it was not simply a matter of noting a few points. The essay may have been off the point. Or perhaps it wasn't clear what she meant by 'comment' on it. In this case it would have been better to email first to ask permission to email the whole assignment.

> Email's easier for me. My English is not great on the telephone but I can check my email message to make sure it says what I want.

This student is making sure she gets her point across.

When writing to your lecturer there may be strict rules about when to send emails and what to write on the subject line. Take a look at this example from one course, shown in Figure 10.

Check first about whether you are allowed to send assignments by email. Not all departments allow this.

Emailing other students

In a previous chapter we talked about making friends with other students. Email is one way of being in touch. Students who feel shy about their spoken English often say that when using email, they feel more confident.

Email language

Email writing is not always easier than other kinds of communication because it can have a language of its own. For example, many messages are

---

All weekly assignments have to be sent before Friday 12:00.

Use the following on the Subject line: week of the course – assignment name
  Example:
  Week 1 – Computer-assisted testing

Guidelines

1. Do not send your assignment in the body of your email, but attach it to the email as a separate file.
2. Do not include questions or comments and other messages in the email body, as these will be discarded. Send them in a separate email.
3. Write a CLEAR SUBJECT to your email. Not something like 'hi!' or 'problem', but write 'When is the next meeting?' or 'Can I get an extension?'
4. Do not send file attachments larger than 300 kb as these get automatically deleted.

Figure 10   Email guidelines

very short, with a minimum of words. To make things more difficult, often words are completely left out and many abbreviations are used that are not used in 'normal' writing, such as

2 = to
4 = for
r = are
u = you

Some teachers think that this short form of spelling will spoil students' written work. However, students who already speak two or three languages say that they know the difference between the language for quick electronic communication with friends and writing for more formal purposes such as essays.

Another way that email language is different is that it can use letters for whole phrases. Some of the most common abbreviations are listed in Table 27.

Table 27 Email abbreviations

Abbreviation	Meaning
FYI	*For your information* Often used at the top of a letter or email. This usually means that the reader doesn't have to do anything with it, but just know it.
BTW	*By the way* Used for something that may or may not be important to the reader, or to give some extra information. *BTW I saw John the other day.*
AFAIK	*As far as I know* This means that you are not 100% sure. *AFAIK he's still in Hong Kong.*
IMO	*In my opinion* This shows the reader that you are not telling a fact but only your opinion. *IMO the assignment question is not clear.*
IMHO	*In my humble opinion* The same as the above but this way you express your opinion carefully or more politely.
HH	*Haha* Laughing
LOL	*Laughing out loud* Used when something is funny, and sometimes when something is not funny but ridiculous.
ROFLOL	*Rolling on the floor laughing out loud* Even funnier!

Table 28 Showing feelings in emails

Emotion	Meaning
S	Smiles
G	Grins
:-) or ☺	Smiles (happy)
;-)	Winks (used when making a joke)
:-(or ☹	Sad or angry
:~(	Sad

In addition, people often use *emoticons* in emails. Emoticons are little face-pictures made out of letters, numbers, or punctuation marks on the keyboard. Table 28 shows you some of them.

For more abbreviations and emoticons you can search the Internet. A good site is:

cckong.xoasis.com/

[Note that this section has been about emailing other students. When you write to your lecturers you don't generally use these personal signs.]

Problems with emails

Although email is less formal than a letter you should still write a well-constructed and polite email. Many people make the mistake of responding to an email quickly when they are happy or angry, and then later they feel sorry about this and wish they could take back their words. Think about your reply to an important message for at least one hour before you send it. Sometimes it's better to leave it until the next day. It is not only *what* you say that you can regret but also *how* you express yourself. It is easy to write something that *sounds* unfriendly even if you do not mean it that way.

Email has rules that make communication easier and more pleasant. These come under what is called 'netiquette', rules about how to use the Internet and when emailing.

For a good introduction to netiquette for email look at this link:

www.library.yale.edu/training/netiquette

Whether you are emailing staff or other students, it's worth remembering that writing emails is very different from writing a letter. It is a bit more like talking to someone. It can be difficult to read emails because many people don't make it clear what they are writing to you about. You can avoid this problem by always writing a clear subject on the subject line:

Don't write: *Subject: hi there!*

But write: *Subject: what's next week's class time?*

In some ways emails are similar to letters. You need to make it clear who you are and what you are writing for. It is not possible for the person you are writing to to ask you what you mean, as in a conversation. Also make sure you are as polite in your emails as in your letters. Because the other person can't see or hear you, it is easy to offend someone. You can show feelings in your emails (see below) but you have to be careful with this. By using asterisks (*) you can emphasise something: 'I *said* that I would come'. Even stronger would be to use capitals: 'I SAID I would come', and using both is strongest: 'I *SAID* I would'. Be careful with all of these as most people will read them as if you are angry.

Finally, to make your emails easier to read on a computer screen you should use more and shorter paragraphs than in a normal letter.

▶ Using a course website

More and more courses now have a website where teachers post messages about the programme and changes in the timetable. Many websites also let students communicate with one another through *discussion boards* and sometimes *chatrooms*. Sometimes these sites are made by the teacher but there are also programs that allow the teacher to use the Internet easily for teaching. Figure 11 is an example of a program called Blackboard, which is used for teaching. The example shows only part of the screen. Many course websites will look like this and have a similar *menu structure*. A menu structure is the set of *hyperlinks* somewhere on the left of the page. You click on a hyperlink to go to a new page. Most course websites will have a menu item

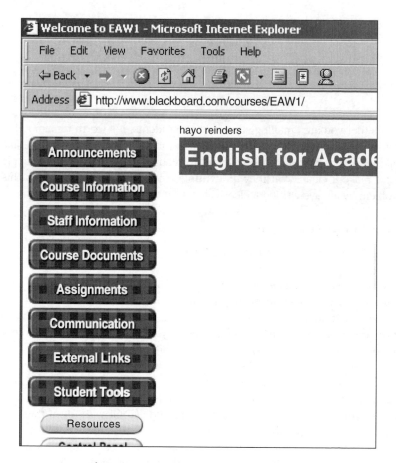

Figure 11 A course website's menu structure

called 'announcements' or something similar where you will read about things like last-minute changes to the programme.

'Course information' tells you what the course is about, who teaches it, at what times you can see the teachers in their offices, and other practical information. 'Assignments' tells you the test dates, the required reading, projects you will be working on, and so on. 'Communication' allows you to send messages to other students and discuss assignments etc. Let's have a closer look. As you can see in Figure 12 you can send emails, see other students' homepages and see group pages. Group pages are useful if you have to work with other students on an assignment because you can then put all your texts and other materials on the group's homepage to share. (See Chapter 5 for more

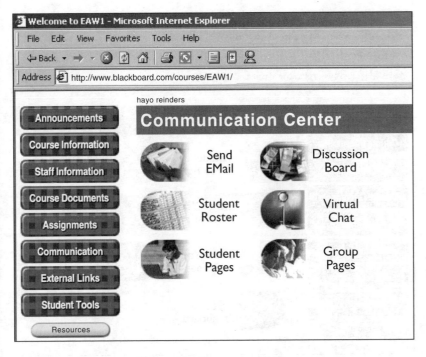

Figure 12   The course website

information on working with other students on joint projects.) 'External links' contains hyperlinks to other information that is useful for the course.

Finally there is a menu item called 'Student Tools'. You can see it in Figure 13. On the Student Tools page you can use a 'student drop box' (on other sites this may be called a 'mailbox' or 'assignment folder' etc.). With this tool you can send files such as essays and assignments to the teacher. Of course you can also use an email program for that, although, as we saw earlier, not all teachers let you do it. Some will still want you to print out your assignments and hand them in.

On this page there is also a calendar where you can keep track of important dates, and a tool that lets you create and change your homepage for other students to see. Finally, 'check your grade' is where you can see your grades. The teacher makes these available here but only you can see your grades.

Discussion boards

Many course websites have a discussion board, where people can post messages and respond to other people's messages. These are a great way

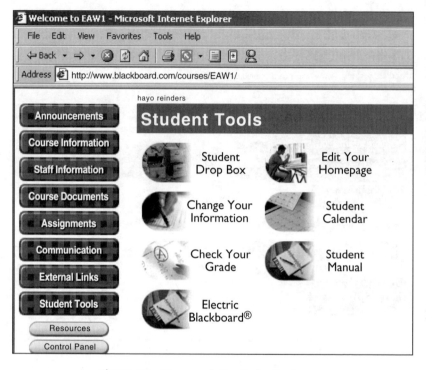

Figure 13   Course website, student tools page

of communicating with other students. Even if your course does not have its own website, it may still use a discussion board somewhere on the Internet.

Several messages about one topic are called a *thread*. Some discussion boards allow any member to start a new thread whereas others only allow one person (such as the teacher) to start one. It is a good idea to check if someone has already started a thread about a topic before starting a new one. You can reply to the person who has started the thread or to the person who has written last.

In Figure 14 you can see an example of how to post a message. 'Post a reply to this message' shows that you are writing in reply to a post on a thread that has already started. You are not making a new thread. For some discussion boards (such as this one) you must have a password and type it in. Usually you type in the subject (topic) of your message and your name. You can add your messages to the thread by clicking on 'send', and by clicking on 'clear' you can start again.

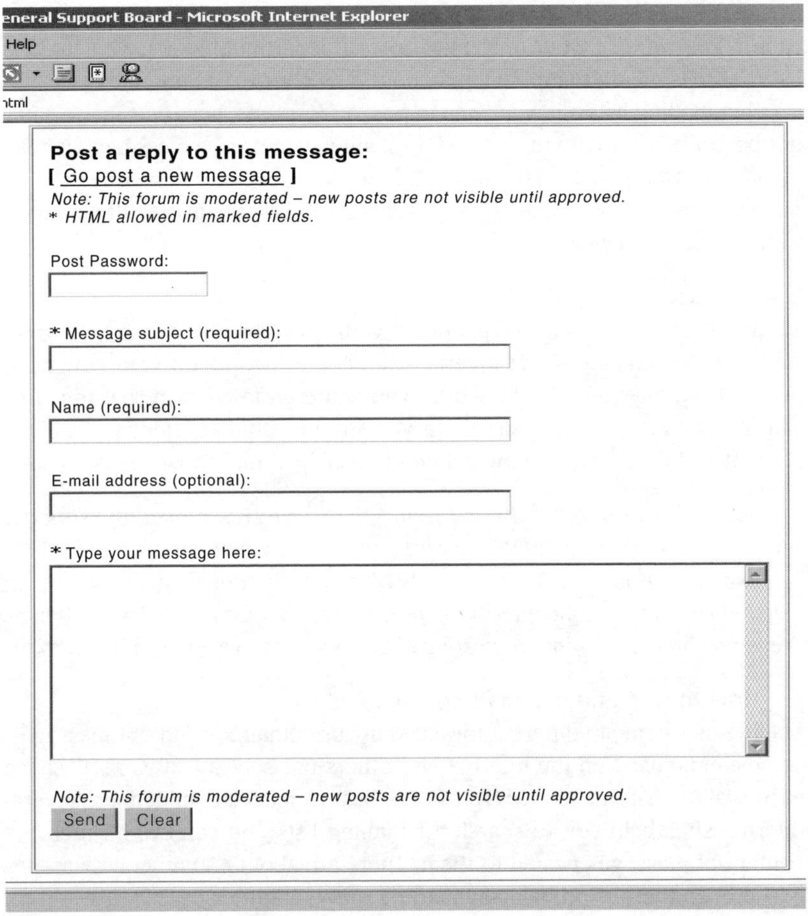

Figure 14 Posting a message

Mailing lists

Discussions with your fellow students are an important source of learning and of making sure you understand course work. Some of these discussions happen through mailing lists.

1. What is a mailing list?

A mailing list is a list of email addresses. People can contact everyone on the list by sending just one email. In other words, if someone sends a message to the list, everyone on that list gets that message.

There are several kinds of mailing lists. One type allows only one person to send messages while everyone else can only receive them. This type of list is usually only to provide information about a topic, not for communication. For example, your university or your department may have a mailing list that tells all staff and students about new courses, exam dates etc.

Other mailing lists allow anyone to post a message. These lists may or may not be *moderated*. With moderated lists, when you send a message it is read by one or more people first, who decide whether or not the message will be posted to the other members. The advantage of this step is that all messages to the list are relevant.

2. Why use mailing lists?

Mailing lists are not only for people at your university. They can be a great way to communicate about a certain topic with people on your course or people from anywhere in the world who share an interest in that topic. As well as being fun, it can also help you in your studies. Here's what one student had to say about how mailing lists helped him to write his thesis.

When I was writing my thesis I found that there was a mailing list about my topic. This was great! Whenever I got stuck or when I needed ideas, help or when I was looking for a certain book or article, somebody would be able to help me. I met some interesting people that I stayed in touch with. Whenever we find something interesting about our topic we let each other know.

3. How to find and use mailing lists

Mailing lists come in different forms. Many use email to send out messages; some can be used on the Internet and others use special software. Because each mailing list has its own rules, it is best to read the guidelines. Several internet sites help you to search for mailing lists and can even search the content of messages posted to them. There are about 650 million messages in there, so there is probably something that will interest you!

Here are two examples.

groups.google.com

A good place to start is this Google site where you can also search the text of sent messages.

www.kovacs.com/cgi-bin/dir1.pl

This site is just for academic lists and lets you search for topics by academic area (e.g. Social Sciences, Arts and Humanities etc.).

Chatrooms

Course websites may also have a chatroom where students communicate with one another about their course, their research, or just for fun! In a chatroom two or more people must be online and visiting the chatroom at the same time. Chatting is like emailing, but the difference is that what you type in is immediately seen by the other and therefore seems very much like talking. There are many advantages to chatting. You have a little bit more time to think about your answers than when you are talking face-to-face and often people use more informal language than when they are writing.

Read instructions carefully as you don't want to send personal or social messages to the whole class. Find out the times when you can chat with staff just by yourself. This is like having an appointment in the lecturer's office. Here are two hints.

1. As with emails, it is easy to sound impolite in email chatting. Usually when we speak face-to-face we use less formal language but we can see the other person's expression and have an idea of what they think. With online chatting we can't see the other person's face and it is easy to sound too direct. Also try not to be more personal than you would in your teacher's office.

2. Perhaps you are nervous about chatting because English is a new language for you, but remember that everyone, including native speakers, makes language mistakes when chatting. For instance, many people seem to type fast without worrying about making spelling mistakes.

Table 29 Common chat abbreviations

Abbreviation	Meaning
BRB	*Be right back* To let the other person/people know that you will be unable to chat for a few minutes. It is like saying 'one minute please' in an ordinary conversation.
BBL	*Be back later* Similar to the above but it means that you will be gone longer.
TTYL	*Talk to you later.*
BFN	*Bye for now.*
CUL	*See you later.*

People generally make a lot of typing mistakes and use abbreviations even more in chatrooms than in emails, so it can make it quite difficult to understand messages sometimes. Some common abbreviations shown in Table 29 are for chatrooms.

Note

1. The source of the extract from the student–teacher interview is: Elizabeth Crandall, 'Native Speaker and Non-native Speaker Requests in an Academic Context'. Occasional Paper no. 12, Department of Applied Language Studies and Linguistics, University of Auckland, 1999.

10 Dealing with Problems

Although this chapter is near the end of the book, perhaps you have turned here first. Through this book we have tried to talk about things going well for you in your studies. However, things can go wrong and being a successful student in another country means dealing with these problems. In this chapter we look at how students have overcome three kinds of problems: problems with studies, social problems and money problems.

> This chapter answers the following questions:
>
> * What sort of problems do university students report?
> * How do students overcome these problems?

▶ Study problems

If you have come from another country you may think that problems about studying are just yours, but many study problems of overseas students are exactly the same as those all students talk about. From time to time everyone worries about managing their time, about finding the right books and articles for essays and even about finding a good place to study. Here are some suggestions for overcoming these problems.

Talk with staff

In the last chapter we suggested talking with staff about problems relating to the course. Perhaps you want advice on how to improve your English or you feel that the course is too difficult for you. Here are some problems that staff have heard.

I feel that my English is weak. I can't understand the lectures.

I took this subject in my country but here we talk about many topics that I haven't heard of before.

I have a lot of trouble writing up my essay because I write very slowly in English. This is my first time studying abroad.

By talking about your problems you are helping the lecturer to understand the problems of other students too. For example, one student said that he had thought the course would be on another topic because he didn't understand the course title. That made the lecturer, and others in that department, think about making course titles clear.

Perhaps you don't want to talk about your worries with your teachers because you feel that the problem is more personal. When the staff member knows you have a problem he or she can direct you to someone who can help. As we saw in the last chapter, universities have people called counsellors who are trained to talk with you about life's problems. Feel free to ask for this extra help.

Read books about how to study

Apart from the book you are reading right now, many other books have been written to help students be better organised with their learning. Here are three you could try.

- Cottrell, Stella (2003) *The Study Skills Handbook*, 2nd edn (Basingstoke: Palgrave-Macmillan).

  This book is in the same series as the book you are reading now and is a good resource to help you develop skills for successful university study.

- Lewis, M. (1999) *How to Study Foreign Languages* (Basingstoke: Macmillan).

  This one is also in the same series you are reading now and is written by one of the authors. It shows you techniques and strategies for learning a foreign language.

- Rubin, J. and I. Thompson (1994) *How to be a More Successful Language Learner* (Boston: Heinle & Heinle).

  Contains great tips on how to learn a language effectively.

There are also some good websites that will give you many tips on how to study. Best of all: the sites listed here are free!

www.skills4study.com

This site has many tips for students on how to organize their studies and learn effectively.

www.ucc.vt.edu/stdysk/stdyhlp.html

This is a very helpful site by the Virginia Polytechnic Institute, with information on things like taking notes, suggestions to improve concentration, etc.

www.iss.stthomas.edu/studyguides

This site contains a lot of study guides and information on strategies for studying, and is an excellent resource.

Ask where to find books and articles

It's easy to think 'Everyone except me knows what to do.' Probably they don't know. Many students wonder where to find books or journals. Ask someone in the library. Do you have a class representative? That person can talk to staff if there is a problem for everyone about finding the right books. Maybe the bookshop needs to order more or maybe the library needs to put books on short loan (see below).

In the library there are general and specialist librarians to help you find the right reading. Don't be afraid of asking questions. That is what librarians are there for. For example, perhaps the computer catalogue tells you that a particular title is in the library and can be borrowed but you can't find it on the shelf. Perhaps it is in 'the short loan collection'.

Ask about places to study

Finding a good place to study can also be a problem. Find out about these places at your university:

the university library;
the department Student Centre;
the Student Association rooms.

Many students also find that their local public libraries have plenty of study space free during the day, although of course they probably don't have the books you want.

▶ Friends and health problems

Other problems are more individual than study problems. We have chosen three major concerns which students and staff report: making and keeping friends, health, and money.

Worries about friends

Friends (or not having them) are among the biggest concerns that students have. This is an even bigger worry for people who have changed countries and lost the company even of people they can say 'hello' to. In the next chapter we have more suggestions about making friends, but here we look at the times when things go wrong with friends.

When we asked students how they had got through times of difficulty with friends, nearly all of them said 'Find someone to talk to.' Nowadays you can communicate with people far away via email and although this is not the same as talking face-to-face it is better than nothing. If you prefer to talk to a stranger, then remember the counsellors. No problem is too big or too small, too simple or too terrible for them. In fact they have probably heard a similar story many times.

Worries about health

Health problems are another type of worry that you need to do something about quickly. Overseas students tell us they are sometimes afraid to go to a Western doctor for various reasons. They might be worried about not being able to explain a problem clearly. They might be afraid of Western medicine and wish they could find a doctor who would give them something more familiar. Some female students don't go to the Student Health Centre in case they have to see a male doctor.

All of these are common worries and the staff at the Student Health Centre will be ready with answers. If they cannot find the right person that day, they might be able to suggest the name of someone else who is suitable for you. In the main Western cities today there are male and female nurses and doctors of many different language and ethnic groups. There is no need to continue with a health problem or think you should wait until the end of the year when you go home. Some health problems can't wait but can easily be cured. Don't worry and worry, before finding this out for yourself.

One thing to consider before you leave home is health insurance. While most English-speaking countries have free services for emergencies like accidents, they may not pay for you to have operations which are not essential but would make your life better.

▶ Money problems

Money (or not having it) is one more thing that can make people anxious. There are some ways around this problem. Ask about some of these possibilities.

A part-time job

If your visa allows it, perhaps you can find some part-time work. It is difficult to balance your need for money with your need to have plenty of time to study, so keep that in mind when you look for extra work. Here are two ideas.

1. Try the Student Union office first. They may have a Student Job Search which matches students with part-time work. Sometimes international students are shocked at the kind of work local students do, such as waiting at tables in a restaurant or pumping petrol. They may be jobs you would never think of doing in your own country but if you really need the money then you could give them a go. You could find them a pleasant change from study.

2. Other jobs might relate to your studies. If you are a senior student you may be able to find work in the university in one of these ways:

    *   part-time work in the university library;
    *   supervising students in the laboratory;
    *   running workshops for students;
    *   selling handbooks at the start of the semester;
    *   taking notes for a student with a disability;
    *   working in one of the bookshops or other shops;
    *   participating in experiments for a university researcher.

An extra allowance

If you have some kind of student allowance from a government or from some other source, it may be that someone could help you to get more. Perhaps you have to pay very high board or rental. If so, it is possible that your housing allowance could go up. Perhaps you are doing a special subject where you need expensive materials. If so, try asking about more money for that.

Hardship grants

Many student associations have something called a 'hardship grant'. This is money which they keep for emergencies. If something sudden and very unexpected happens to you, perhaps you can be helped from this money. For example, perhaps the accommodation you had comes to an end suddenly and you need money for another place.

This last chapter has been short and has, perhaps, not covered all the topics you wanted, but the main message is this. Everyone, from time to time, has worries about their own lives. When you are in a new country without your family and your good friends, these problems can be worse, especially if you don't want to worry your family at home with these problems. The important thing when you have worries is to talk with someone. Whether your worries are about your study, or your life, or your money, here are the people to think about talking with: your friends; your supervisor/tutor; the international advisor; the university counsellor.

11 Life Beyond Lectures

So far this book has been mainly about your studies. This final chapter is about other things you need to know when you start university in a new country. For example, there is information about the titles and jobs of people who work at a university. This chapter also discusses what we call 'university culture', namely the way people behave in Western universities and how systems may differ from other systems you are familiar with. There are also suggestions for contacting other students and making new friends.

This chapter answers the following questions:

- Where do you find university staff?
- What's different about life at an English-speaking university?
- How do students get to know one another?
- How can students meet people outside the university?

▶ University culture: What's different?

This section starts by talking about culture in general. We then discuss ways that universities are different from other places of study, such as schools. In this chapter you will find answers to these questions:

- What is culture?
- How is a university culture different from a school culture?
- How might English-language universities differ from universities in your country?

In the English-speaking world, universities have many traditions which are the same from one country to another. However, detailed answers to the questions listed above change from one university to another and even from one part of the university to another. For example, lectures and tutorials could have different forms in science, architecture, English literature or language, law, medicine and so on. In one department students may take plenty of notes during lectures while in another the lecturer gives full notes at the end. In one department the custom may be that students prepare for tutorials but in another the discussion topic is not given until the tutorial starts.

What is culture?

We talk about belonging to a particular culture, but what does the word mean? 'Culture' can refer to any of these:

old buildings which tourists love to photograph;
people dancing in traditional clothes;
religious beliefs that go back hundreds of years;
books and music that belong to particular language groups.

One meaning of 'culture' is a group of people with the same language, beliefs and history but the word can also mean a group of people who belong together in some way. That second meaning is the one we use in this chapter. Let's start by thinking of smaller cultural groups that you know already. How many of these cultural groups do you feel you belong to?

people who like the same type of music;
speakers of your language or your dialect;
people who play the same sport as you.

When you are with these people you act like them in various ways, such as:

the way you talk to one another;
the jokes you enjoy;
the things you do in your spare time.

When we talk about the culture of the university we mean the things that make universities different from other places of learning, such as schools, and from other groups of people, such as colleagues at a place of work.

Comparing school and university cultures

Let's start by comparing the cultures of universities and high schools. In Table 30 there are some differences you will find. Let's see what some of these differences mean in detail.

Teachers and students

At high school, teachers notice if students are late to class or absent and want to know a reason. In fact they often keep a roll, particularly in junior

Table 30   Comparing school and university

Differences	High school	University
Students' independence	School responsible for students. Teachers supervise activities. Attendance noted. Teachers guide homework.	Students independent. Students organise clubs. Attendance not noted. Students plan own assignments.
Teaching styles	Varies from class to class.	Lecture style.
Assignments	Shorter.	Longer.
Students' age	Similar ages in one class.	All ages in one class.

classes. If you are absent at university you will probably not be missed in the big first-year classes. Lecturers might notice people walking in late but usually they don't say anything.

There are only a few times when the lecturer might say something about students' behaviour. Probably the most frequent one is when they ask students to turn off their cellphones, especially after one has rung in the middle of a lecture. Another time is if some students talk noisily during the lecture. Otherwise students are in charge of their own behaviour and will sometimes ask other students to keep quiet.

Teaching styles
In high school there are great differences in the way teachers teach, but generally they take time to check if students have understood, by asking questions. At university the staff do their best to make new ideas clear, but they don't say the same thing over and over until everyone understands. As we saw in Chapter 4 they may ask if people understand, but it is up to the students to answer.

Assignments
At school you had homework after every class and this may or may not have counted for your end-of-year results. By contrast, in most universities today, every assignment you do counts for your final results. That is why it is important to have a medical certificate if you are ill and miss an assignment or have to hand work in late.

Outside class
High school teachers are interested in out-of-class activities like sport and drama. As you will know, if you left the school grounds during the day you

had to get permission. At university, once you walk out of the lecture or tutorial your time is your own. You can go to the library and study, you can go
to the cafeteria and meet friends or you can lie on the grass and go to sleep.
Whatever you do, your lecturers will not interrupt you.

The age of students
School students are usually about the same age in each class but at university you will notice that students are of all ages. Many students start a degree
or return to university later in life.

One student's story
As well as differences between school and university, there are differences
between university cultures from one country to another. The student who
tells the story below found many differences between studying in his own
country (Holland) and studying in Syria. After each part of his story, there is
a chance for you to make your own comparison. We give some information
about practices in 'Western', English-speaking universities and then there is
a space for you to put what you think about a system you are accustomed to.

1. *Some students were an hour early to get a seat close to the lecturer.
   When I came in people looked surprised. Kindly they made room for
   me at one of the tables close to the lecturer's stand.*

'Western' university	**Your school or university**
Students arrive at the last minute.	
They sit wherever they want.	

2. *When the lecturer came in everybody got up and greeted him.*

'Western' university	**Your school or university**
Nobody stands for the lecturer.	
The lecturer might say 'Good morning'	
but students don't usually answer.	

3. *Once the lecturer started his lecture he never stopped. There was no
   introduction about what was going to be covered, no summary of what*

the previous lecture had been about. He mainly told in his own words what could be found in the course book.

'Western' university   **Your school or university**

Lecturers say at the beginning
  what they will be talking about.
They usually pause from time to
  time.
The lecture covers more than just
  the textbook.

---

4. *Some students asked questions about the lecturer's opinion about a certain topic, something that wouldn't happen often in my country where the lecturer is usually expected to be objective and not share his personal opinions too much, at least not in lectures. Some of the questions were obviously intended to allow the lecturer to show off his vast knowledge of the topic.*

'Western' university   **Your school or university**

Students usually ask about
opinions in tutorials, not in lectures
  (see Ch. 5).
If students do ask questions it is
  because they want an answer.

---

5. *Occasionally a student would get up and start what seemed like a short presentation on the topic, almost repeating what the lecturer had just said.*

'Western' university   **Your school or university**

Only lecturers stand at the front
  and talk. Students present their ideas
  in seminars, not in lectures.

---

6.   *No one ever disagreed with the lecturer, which also was quite different from what I was used to.*

'Western' university   **Your school or university**
People don't usually disagree
with the lecturer in the middle of a
lecture but they might have a
discussion later in the tutorial
or even one-to-one.

---

7.   *I found out that many students used the lectures to avoid having to read the book, as a sort of human audio cassette. Memorisation was very important and some students remembered whole pages of text.*

'Western' university   **Your school or university**
Students need to read the textbook
as well as attending lectures.

Students would find it very difficult to
learn pages of the textbook by heart.

Students talk about their own countries

Readers from different countries will recognise some things about this student's story but they will also notice differences. Here are questions and answers from students of many nationalities who were asked about the culture of their countries. Thinking about your own culture will help prepare you for similarities and differences.

1.   What do people think about teachers in your country?

   Teachers are important people in society.
   Teachers know the answers to all students' questions.
   The job of a teacher is to make students learn.

2.   In your country, how do students pass their courses?

   They go to all the classes.
   They learn information by heart.
   They have one examination at the end of the year.

3. What happens during lectures?

    The lecturer give students all the information about the subject.
    Lecturers speak slowly like a dictation.
    Students write down everything the lecturer says.

4. Apart from lectures, what do students learn from?

    One textbook has everything for each course.
    The lecturer hands out notes for students to learn from.
    We copy the notes of the best students in the class.
    We can't borrow library books. We take notes from them in the library.

Comparisons with 'Western' universities

Now let's make more comparisons between your answers and answers you could hear if you asked the same questions about English-speaking universities.

What do people think about teachers?

Teachers in English-speaking universities are usually called 'lecturers' or 'tutors' but students often call them by their first names. In society they are usually seen as no better or worse than anyone else. Western students certainly do not believe that university lecturers know all the answers.

We asked some university staff and students to say what they thought the teacher's role was. Here are their answers, starting with the staff.

Lecturer 1

When I started out I was a tutor and then I thought my job was to make clear what the lecturers had said in their lectures. Then when I became a lecturer myself I thought it was really for me to make myself clear the first time without leaving it to tutors later in the week.

Lecturer 2

My work is making the subject interesting for the people who want to learn. My sister's a secondary school teacher and she says her work includes making people learn but I think at university it's more up to the students. They have paid their fees. If they want to learn that's good and I'm there to help them but if they fall asleep in class I never wake them up.

This is what two students said:

Student 1

Our tutors say they are there to teach us how to find answers to questions ourselves.

Student 2

> *I come to a lecture for a purpose. I want to learn more about that topic. It all depends on what I have learned before and where I'm going in the future. The lecturer doesn't know what subjects I'll be specialising in next year and doesn't have to. I see him/her as someone who can guide me to the information that I need.*

How do students pass their courses?

In English-speaking universities attending lectures every week and doing the final examination is not enough. You must also do assignments, whatever form they take. There will usually be in-class tests as well. In general, you need to show an understanding of the subject and, in some professional courses, that you can apply it. In other words, you can use your knowledge in a new situation.

Lecturers introduce a subject and then tell students where to find more information by themselves. Students take notes but don't write down everything that is said.

What happens during lectures?

See Chapter 4 for information about what happens during lectures.

What do students learn from?

Students learn in various ways. They go to the library to find information, to use the Internet, and to borrow resources to take home and study further. As well as the lectures and assignments that we have already talked about, they go to tutorials where they learn in small groups. Out-of-class discussions with other students are also an important part of learning.

The university culture is not only about studying. As you will see in this next section, making friends is one important way of starting to feel at home in a new place.

▶ Making friends

A university can seem a very unfriendly place. Students hurry along with their books and papers looking busy, or sit for hours talking to their friends. At first it can look as if there is no place for someone who has no friends. Although it is easy to think that everyone else is happy and in groups, that may not be the case. The students you see hurrying to their lectures or tutorials or the library could be feeling quite lonely. Even students who study in their own country can feel very lonely in their first few weeks at university. They too ask questions like these:

Will I be able to make friends?
Do people talk to strangers at university?

The answer to these questions is 'Yes' but making real friends can take time. You want to do well in your studies but you also want to be happy socially. This section is about making friends.

Comparing two countries

Although many students can feel lonely even in their own country, there are some reasons why many international students do not find it easy to make friends immediately. Table 31 summarises some differences between two countries we are calling A and B. A is an English-speaking country and B is a mixture of features of several countries.

Suggestions from students

The differences we have described need not be a barrier to finding friends. Here are some ways that students say they made friends.

Student 1

I was standing outside the room waiting for the first lecture and I saw hundreds of other students standing around too. Maybe there weren't hundreds but that's the way it looked to me. I was pretty sure this was the right room but I felt lonely so I asked another student if this was the room for the . . .

Table 31   Differences between countries

	Country *A*	Country *B*
Study	Students work as individuals.	Students work in groups.
Feelings	Students may put personal feelings into words to other students.	Students share their feelings with only one or two friends.
Leadership	One person often offers to lead a group.	Everyone waits to be asked to lead.
Speaking	People speak quietly in public.	People speak loudly in public.
Going out	Male and female students go out together in the daytime or at night.	Male and female students don't spend time together freely. They come home early at night.
Love	Love relationships can begin easily and are not a secret.	Love relationships start more slowly and are often kept secret.

lecture. Maybe she was lonely too. I don't know about that but she did talk on and on and we sat together, so that was one person I could talk to.

Student 2

We were queuing up to get a signature for our courses. Nobody was saying anything and some of them were looking a bit stressed because it was hot but then one student started making jokes and others joined in. After a while lots of people were talking to one another.

Student 3

The cafeteria was a good place to meet people. The tables were usually over-flowing and people would ask if they could sit at your table. Sometimes the talk went from there. Sometimes it didn't.

Student 4

I went to study in Syria, in the Middle East. Friends who had been there before recommended I should live in the old city rather than in one of the suburbs where many foreigners tend to go and where they live in large houses and have little contact with the Syrian people. After coming to the old city I asked around and was finally directed to some houses where they accepted foreigners to come for a homestay. That turned out to be a good way to get used to the language.

Student 5

I was complaining to my grandmother about all the queues for enrolling. She said, 'You wouldn't be alive today if it wasn't for university queues. That's where I met your grandfather.'

Not everyone will have these particular experiences but here are some general guidelines for making friends at university.

* Any student can speak to any other student.
* Start talking about general things: the weather, the food, the lecture.
* Wait to ask really personal questions until you know people better.
* Males and females can speak to each other.

Some students join an overseas students' club. This can be a good idea because all the students there are from another country and, like yourself, probably don't know many people. On the other hand, you will probably not meet many locals there, and wasn't that one of the reasons for going overseas?

Culture and politeness
Rules of politeness differ from one culture to another. Listen to conversations around the university and think about these questions.

1. In a conversation between students, which is more common?
    People wait a few seconds between speakers.
    Everyone speaks quickly one after the other.

2. When students want to refuse something, which is more common?
    They say 'no thank you' clearly.
    They find an excuse for saying 'no'.

3. In groups of students, who usually speaks first?
    The older person or the younger person?
    Males or females?
    The senior student or the junior student?

These are just a few examples; there are no fixed ways of behaving. When you are studying with people from many different countries you will become accustomed to many different ways of doing things and many different ways of speaking.

Friends and spending money
You will find big differences in how much money students can spend on food and entertainment. If someone says 'No thanks' when you ask them to join you and your friends for a meal, maybe they are worried about how much it will cost. If you are the one who is being careful with your money then you could suggest other activities such as:

Going to the beach to go swimming or surfing.
Going for a walk away from the city.
Having a picnic.
Visiting a museum.
Meeting in a coffee shop.

One way to start talking is to meet the person who has been voted as the class representative (or 'class rep.' for short). (Occasionally, instead of voting, someone might just say 'I'll do it,' and that's it. Everyone else is so pleased that someone is willing to do the job that they don't ask any questions.) Speak to the rep. if you have problems with the course and this person can then talk to the staff on behalf of all the students in the class. For example, here are the things that one group of class reps mentioned at a meeting with staff.

1. Does this class have to be at that time of day? We would rather have a different time.
2. We have a problem finding the set books in the library.
3. Can we have a different classroom? That one's not comfortable.

Finally, don't keep only to the people who are like you. Think of all the groups you could be meeting:

Science students, Arts students, Architecture students etc.;
international students, local students;
school leavers, mature age students;
first-, second-, third-year students.

You will meet all of these students on your courses, in your lectures and tutorials or in other parts of university life.

▶ Life outside university

So far we have discussed life inside the university. To finish this chapter and book we talk about non-university life in your new country. Although some people spend their whole lives with other students, others who have made an effort to join the wider community say they have found fresh interests and people there.

Finding somewhere to live

You have a number of choices for accommodation. Here are five ideas.

1. Homestays

A homestay means living with a family. People choose a homestay if they want to use English every day and improve their speaking and listening or if they want to meet local families. Being in a homestay means sharing a house with at least one adult and sometimes children as well. Homestay students eat with the family and sometimes share in the household tasks. The arrangements are usually made by a company which is part of the university or by an agent in your own country.

Homestays can work very well, as shown by these comments from two students:

Student 1

To me it was an excellent way to see how people in that country lived. I was lucky because they were very kind to me and took me around and showed me places, especially in the first few weeks when I didn't know anyone yet.

Student 2

It really helped me to improve my English! In the beginning I felt quite shy and it was easier to talk to my homestay family then to strangers. Also, I learned a lot of English that I hadn't heard before like local expressions etc.

The host families have their opinions too.

Example 1

We really enjoyed the Japanese student who stayed with us. She was willing to join in our family life and we often invited her to go out with us at the weekends.

Occasionally, though, the student and family do not seem to enjoy the arrangement. Here is a comment from the same host mother.

Example 2

Unfortunately the last student we had shut herself in her room all the time except for meals. She wouldn't join in activities with us and she didn't seem to have any student friends either. We felt she would have been better mixing with other people.

Think about a homestay. If you would rather spend your time alone studying then you can find a cheaper arrangement. It may not be too difficult to change the arrangement if you are not happy but you should talk about whether this is possible *before* you sign on.

2. Boarding houses

In boarding houses each student has a bedroom but shares the kitchen and bathroom with a number of others. If students want to, they can talk with one another, but if they prefer to be alone that is easy too. In some cities, old homes near the university have been turned into boarding houses or new buildings have been specially constructed. These are usually cheaper than a homestay.

If you plan to live in a boarding house you will probably want to visit it first. People who like this arrangement say it can be quite cheap, but people who don't like it say that the standard of these buildings can vary. In other words, some are quite old and not well maintained while others may be new but very, very small. Also if you are ill, nobody will take any notice of you unless you have made friends with the other students.

3. Hostels

In a hostel you have your own bedroom, but someone else prepares your meals and these are served at fixed times. Hostels are usually more expensive than boarding, but if they are close to the university you will save money on public transport. The cost of the hostel usually includes all your meals, or perhaps just breakfast and the evening meal. You may be able to cut down the cost by doing extra duties such as cleaning or answering the telephone at fixed times. Because hostels are quite popular, you would probably need to book your place before arriving in the country.

4. Flatting

Flatting means sharing a house or a flat with other students. The house may be an old one divided into flats, or a building specially built for flats. Flats are owned by landlords, and the landlords like a regular arrangement for paying, such as having automatic payments from your bank account to theirs.

Finding other students to flat with is difficult when you have just arrived, but you will probably find a few other students to share with before long. One way of doing this is by looking at the noticeboard in the Students' Association building. There you will see notices like this one in a British university:

Flatmate Wanted

Friendly, easy-going flatmate (M/F) wanted who would like to share meals and good times with us – 2 guys and 2 girls, in a Central appt w garden. Close to bus. £90 p wk + expenses

---

One problem you can see immediately is understanding all the abbreviations in these advertisements. If the advertisement is in a newspaper you will need to look at the part of the newspaper where they explain them, or ask a local person. In the example above:

M/F = male or female
appt = apartment
w   = with
p wk = per week

Once you have found people to flat with, the arrangements can vary enormously. Here are some questions that students usually talk about beforehand:

Do we cook meals together or separately?
If we prepare them together do we take turns?
Do people with bigger rooms pay more rent than others?
How do we know who spent what at the supermarket?
Does the landlord want the rent together or separately?
If (s)he wants it together then who is responsible for collecting it?

5. Living alone

To live alone means that you need enough money to rent your own flat, apartment or house. This can, of course, be more expensive than flatting with others but it suits people who have enough money and who are very independent. The way to find a flat is to look in one of these places:

the newspaper;
the Students' Association noticeboard;
the student noticeboard;
a real-estate agent's office.

Travelling to university

When you are thinking about where to live, at the same time you could think about how you will get from your living place to the university. Here are some questions to help you to decide.

Is there good, frequent transport at all hours?
How expensive is transport?
Do students have special rates?
Is it easy to walk to the university?
What about walking around the streets at night?

Some students in English-speaking countries buy their own cars. Of course whether you choose to do this depends on a number of things, including parking. Does the university have free student carparks? A car is expensive to run. Check the price of petrol and repairs before you buy your own car. A cheap old car may not be cheap if you are always paying for repairs, because in most English-speaking countries the people who repair cars have quite a good income.

Joining the wider community

In your own country you will have been part of many groups of people. First there was your family and then there were your schoolfriends. You were probably also part of wider groups that covered all age groups. Here are some groups you could be interested in outside the university.

Sports and hobbies

If you have a sporting or hobby interest that could help you be part of the wider community, look in the newspaper, especially smaller local newspapers, to find out where these groups meet. Music and chess groups, to name just two, are part of most local communities.

Voluntary groups

In every community there are groups of people who offer their time free to others. One overseas student found herself pouring cups of tea one morning a week for people with disabilities. Through that work she came to know many of the other volunteers.

Places of worship

If you usually attend a mosque, temple, synagogue or church then have a look in the paper to see advertisements for these. As well as being places where you can continue with your faith, these places could put you in touch with families who are very welcoming to overseas students. Here is what one student found.

> *At home I always went to the . . . once a week. When I got to . . . I went to the nearest . . . but I saw that it was full of other international students. I didn't want that. I wanted to meet local people. Anyway, I asked a few people and they said 'You should go to . . .' It was only one bus ride away so I went there and found some friendly people. Especially people with little children were good to me. I played with the children and they didn't mind about my English.*

Be like this student. If at first you don't find the right place, try again.

In this chapter we have tried to show a picture of university life outside class and we have given you some examples from students' experiences. If you go straight from school in your own country to university somewhere else, then of course there will be many, many unusual things to find out about. As we have seen, there is no short way of saying exactly how one university will seem to you.

We hope that this chapter has been a help to you in finding out about differences and being ready for them. There may be difficulties but there is also support for you. The most common answer to 'What makes the difference between feeling lonely and feeling happy' is 'communication'.

Glossary:
A Mini-dictionary of
University Words

This final section is a list of words that have been used in this book, or that you may encounter at university, with their meanings. When you first arrive at a new university you will hear many new words and phrases. Some of them refer to people, some to places and some to parts of your courses. The terms in the following list are particularly common in universities which follow the British tradition. You will find differences in places where they use American terms.

Word	Meaning
Additional or recommended reading	Extra books and articles suggested by the lecturer for your course reading
Aegrotat pass	An examination pass for someone who is too ill to take the examination. Aegrotat passes may be given to students who have done well through the rest of the course
Assessment	The way students' work is measured (assignments, tests, examinations)
Assignments	Students' essays, projects etc. which count for the course grade
Attachment	A file that comes with an email
Boolean operators	Words you can use to make your Internet search more specific
Brainstorming	Thinking of many ideas for a piece of writing
Breaks (mid- or inter-semester breaks)	The weeks when there are no lectures
Calendar	The book that lists all official university information
Campus	All the university buildings and grounds

Word	Meaning
Catalogue, online catalogue	A list of all the books in the library
CEO (chief executive officer)	The leader of a university or polytechnic. (Most universities use the term 'vice chancellor'.)
Certified copies	A signed piece of paper which says the paper is a true copy of the original
Chaplaincy	The people who are interested in students' spiritual life
Conjoint degree	A degree from two different university faculties. It takes longer than one degree but not as long as two.
Co-requisites	Two different courses which must be taken at the same time are called co-requisites
Counsellors	Staff who listen to students' problems
Course reader	Articles and/or chapters on the topic, photocopied and bound together for students on a course
Credit	Points towards a degree for a course you have taken at another university
Criteria (*singular*: criterion)	What you need before you can do something else (e.g. 'There are 3 criteria for getting into this course.')
Database	A collection of information, usually on a computer
Dean	The head of the Faculty
Degree	a BSc, a BA, a BCom, etc.
Degree programme	All the courses you take to make up your degree
Department	One part of the university, e.g. the History Department
Deputy vice-chancellor	The person who works with the vice-chancellor but at a sightly lower level

Word	Meaning
Diagnostic test	A test to tell students what they are good and not so good at
Draft	A copy you write of an assignment or an article before the final copy
Edited book	A book with chapters from more than one author
E-journals	Electronic journals that you can find and read on a computer
Eligible	Able to do something, e.g. eligible for a course
Emoticon	Little face-pictures like these: ☺ or ;-)
Exchange programme	Students from two countries each do some study in the other's country.
Exemptions/exempt	Permission not to take a compulsory subject. If you know a language very well you may be exempt from the first-year course
Facilities	Places (libraries, computer rooms) and things (photocopiers) that students can use
Faculty	A large part of a university where similar types of subjects are taught. A faculty is a larger grouping than a department.
Foundation studies programme	A course for students who are not yet ready to enter the university
GPA	The marks you have already got for your previous study
Graduation ceremony	The occasion when you receive your degree
Handouts	Pages of information used in a course
HoD	Head of Department
IELTS	International English Language Testing System
Index	An alphabetical list of words, and the pages where they appear, at the end of a book

Word	Meaning
International Baccalaureat	A school-leaving examination which is recognised all over the world
International Office	The place where staff look after overseas students
Justice of the Peace	A person who is legally allowed to sign documents
Keyword	A word you use on a computer to search for the topic you want
Language conversation exchange	You teach your language; the other student teaches you his/her language
Learning journals	A book where you write about your studies
Literature	1. The novels, plays, poems etc. of a country or language 2. Books and articles on a particular academic subject
Mailing list	A list that people subscribe to so that they can exchange messages with anyone on the list, usually about a certain topic
Major	A main subject
Minor	A subject studied for only one or two years
Moderated discussion list	A computer address list where messages are first read by one or more people before they are sent to everyone on the list
Needs analysis	A way of finding out what your weaknesses are and what you need to improve first
Orientation Day	The time at the beginning of the year when students are welcomed to the university
PhD	The highest degree at a university
Portfolio	A collection of work in one subject as part of the course assessment, e.g. an art portfolio
Prefix	The first part of a word which has a meaning of its own (e.g. *pre*-departure)

Word	Meaning
Prerequisites	Courses you must study before you can enrol in a course or programme
Prescribed/required reading, reading list	Books and articles that you must read for your course
Proficiency	Being good at something
Provisional entrance	Permission to start university study without the right qualifications. Students with provisional entrance who do well continue to study at the university
Reference books	Books which students may read in the library but not take away
References	A list of everything read and used in a book, article or essay
Research article	A piece of writing, in a journal, about some original work
Scholarship	Money to help students with their study
Semesters	The two or three parts of the university year
Seminars	Times when students present their work orally
Short-loan collection	Books which may be borrowed for a short time only
Spellchecker	A function of a computer program that checks your document for spelling and grammar mistakes
State-of-the-art or review article	An article which sums up what other people have written on a topic
Study break	Time without lectures when students prepare for examinations
Supervisor	The lecturer who guides you as you write your thesis or dissertation
Teaching assistants (TA)	(Mostly postgraduate) students who teach (part of) a course

Word	Meaning
Thesaurus	A book which lists words of similar meaning
Thesis	Original work by one student for a postgraduate degree
Thread	Messages about one topic on a discussion board
TOEFL	Test of English as a Foreign Language
Truncate	To shorten, e.g. very long emails may be truncated
Tutorials	Times when small groups of students and their tutor talk about the course content
(Under)graduate advisor	Someone who helps students plan their first degree
Undergraduates	Students who have not yet received a diploma or a degree
Vice-chancellor	The leader (or 'head') of a university
Voicemail	A telephone answering machine. You can leave a message on someone's voicemail

Index